Coaching the
Spread Bone Offense
Spread the Field

Heath Hamrick
Todd Allen

COACHES ≡ CHOICE™

ISBN: 1-58518-956-1
Library of Congress Control Number: 2005938996
Cover design: Jeanne Hamilton
Book layout: Shannon Popp
Diagrams: Deborah Oldenburg
Front cover photo: Ronald Martinez/Getty Images

Coaches Choice
P.O. Box 1828
Monterey, CA 93942
www.coacheschoice.com

"Inflexibility. It was the worst human failing; you could learn to check impetuosity, you could overcome fear through confidence and laziness through discipline, but rigidity of mind allowed for no antidote. It carried the seeds of its own destruction."

—Anton Myrer
Once An Eagle

"It is only natural to prefer the rising sun to one that sets."

—Gnaeus Pompeius Magnus

Dedication

For my loving family, my beautiful and supportive wife, Keri, and my true inspiration: a high school coach both loved and respected and who remains my coach still—my father, Slugger Hamrick.
—Heath Hamrick

For my parents, who allowed me to waste literally thousands of dollars of their money in pursuit of various ventures, all of which have led me to this point. Your patience and acceptance of everything I've done is deeply appreciated. For my wife, Morgan, whose job has no guidelines, no boundaries, and horrible hours. You amaze me; your tolerance, patience, and love of all things that comprise me are infinite. In short, Morgan, this book is for you most of all.
—Todd Allen

...faith in the face of doubt.

Table of Contents

Introduction:
Catching the Chameleon

Any good coach will tell you that the key to success in the game of football is observation. Whether it be the observations of a coaching staff while breaking down game film, a coordinator recognizing coverages and tendencies from the box, or a player picking up on the differences between the opposing noseguard playing outside eye or straight up, the cornerstone of football lies not in violence, but in observance. As this book has been written with coaches in mind, let's practice that crucial skill and make an observation together.

Pick a town or city anywhere in America. It makes little difference whether it's a thriving metropolis or the smallest of oil-field towns. Now wait until mid-August, until coaches start filing into dingy offices at ungodly hours, until players start strapping on new equipment, and until the whole community catches its collective breath in anticipation. Wait until the sportswriters have had a chance to interview the head coaches after the first week of two-a-days, and until the photographers have had a chance to snap a team photo. In most towns, large or small, the weekend after the first two-a-days finds an added section placed in each newspaper. We all know what these sections contain: a preview of the upcoming season, with each local team properly interviewed, photographed, catalogued, pigeon-holed, and judged according to the best educated guess of the media.

Now that you've got this rather bulky section of the newspaper in your hand, notice, if you will, that one of the most basic pieces of information given about a team is its offensive set. As football is just as much about gambling as it is about observation, let's make a bet together. I'll bet that 75% of those teams are running an offense called the spread. Chances are you've heard of it. Chances are equally good that what you've heard is dead wrong.

I first became aware of the spread while I was in high school in a small town called Bremond, nestled on the edge of the Texas Hill Country. At that time, another small school in the area caught the excitement of the state by running a high-powered offensive attack out of wide-open sets, setting passing records at a record pace with athletes no one thought capable of any great success. In that year, the Rogers Eagles and their vaunted "Black Gun" offense, under the lead of Coach Joel Berry, plowed their way into the state finals before finally losing to Stanford.

The accomplishments of the Rogers Eagles set the state on fire, causing the fans, coaches, players, and media in the area to examine and praise this "new" offense in utter excitement.

Eight years later, the wide-open, high-scoring potency of the Roger's offense is a commonplace sight on Friday nights, and the spread has become the latest effort in the sport's driving need to find "the perfect scheme." The spread offense is being seen more and more at the high school levels as coaches realize that it can be run with exciting results without college-caliber athletes. It is truly the "hot" topic at any coaching clinic or passing camp. It is the offense that everyone who's anyone is incorporating into their package. Which is not to say that the spread is a new concept; like most things considered "cutting-edge," the spread has been around, in one form or another, for quite awhile. In fact, for years almost every coach in America could tune in to the NFL on Sundays and see the spread in action. They just didn't know it.

The spread is elusive prey, a perfect offensive chameleon that, when properly implemented, gives away nothing of the forthcoming action from the mere formation. In this aspect, it is different from many offensive sets. The spread is not a formation, like the wishbone or the power-I, despite what you may have heard. It a common misconception among coaches that a spread offense runs exclusively out of one formation, the five-wide, or "empty," set. Nothing could be further from the truth. The spread is not a five-wide set. It is not a doubles or trips set. It incorporates many one-back formations into a cohesive and powerful offensive philosophy, an entire mindset, which a coach can utilize to shred opposing defenses and rack up yardage, points, and victories. I cannot emphasize this point enough—the spread is not a formation, it is an offensive philosophy.

It is also commonly thought that the spread is for teams with young, arrogant, hotshot coaches who want to throw the ball 60 times a game whether they have the athletes or not. The truth is that one-back sets have traditionally been used as passing formations, giving the quarterback as many passing options as possible. Running plays have often been limited to simple draws, counters, and, more recently, the speed option. However, the years of innovation by coaches nationwide, and our experiences on the field, have led us to the realization that the spread, or, specifically, the spread bone, can be just as devastating a ground attack as anything run out of traditional run-oriented sets. In fact, with the proper mindset, proper tools, and the proper preparation, the spread can enable a team to be equally deadly on the ground as in the air.

"Spread" is not a magic word, however. Calling your offense the spread does not guarantee you an explosive result. The harsh reality is that most so-called spread teams are flailing about in the dark, cognizant enough to realize the spread's enormous potential but unprepared to implement it to its full effectiveness. It is important to realize that the spread is a weapon, the most potent offensive armament the game has yet seen, and, like all weapons, it can be confusing, ineffective, and even dangerous to those who don't know how to use it. Coaches who seek to run "a little spread" in their offenses will find that the attempt backfires. Without understanding the underlying assumptions and mental attitude of the spread, attempts to utilize a spread game plan will meet with infrequent success. Thus, the goal of this book is to familiarize coaching professionals with all the tools they need to run an effective spread offense. In the following chapters we will outline the plays, philosophy, and coaching attitude needed to implement the most versatile, most powerful, and most aggressive offense ever conceived.

Know Your Chosen Weapon

"There comes a time in every man's life when he must spit on his hands, hoist the black flag, and start slitting throats."

—H.L. Mencken

In fencing, a sport that, like football, resembles that most ancient sport of all—warfare—there exists a tradition of the search for the perfect thrust, the attack that absolutely cannot be parried. The spread has often been likened to the perfect offense, a package that no defense can stop. While amateurs may tout a particular lunge or play as perfect, professionals have long realized that the perfect thrust and the perfect offense are unattainable ideals and unreachable goals. Like Alexander the Great, those who seek after the ghosts of perfection will always fall a bit short. It is in the striving, however, that greatness is achieved, whether on the gridiron or the battlefield, and the coaching profession's continual struggle with X's and O's has led it to the spread—Babylon at the end of a long journey.

When you take a foil or an epee blade in your hand, you cannot seek to deliver the perfect thrust, but you can seek to perfectly execute the talents at your disposal. The same concept applies to the football field. Perfect execution relies on perfect understanding, in this case a perfect knowledge of the spread—what it is, what it does, and what to do with it. After knowledge comes application, the plays and diagrams that make up the bulk of this book.

Many coaches in the position to control their own offense have been in the business long enough to have already set their notions of an offensive philosophy, and may be tempted to skip this chapter. This is a mistake. Knowing how to fire a double-barreled shotgun doesn't give a person the know-how to operate an Apache helicopter, though their basic missions are the same. This analogy carries over into football in that knowing how to run the wishbone doesn't mean a person knows how to run the spread, though both offenses have the same overall goal—to score.

First, a clarification: unlike most other offensive schemes, no set and accepted way to run the spread exists. Almost any offense characterized by one-back sets, whether devoted to the pass or to the run, is generically called the spread. Naturally, this has led to a great deal of confusion for coaches who want to utilize this type of offense. Many coaches have no guide for the motivations or goals, or a proper philosophy, of the spread offense. Most approach this fact as a challenge, and as a result a multitude of diverse offenses are running out of one-back sets. A handful of coaches have achieved great success, while many, many more are not seeing the offensive payoff they anticipated.

The version of the spread outlined in this book has arisen from one of the most common complaints leveled at spread offenses, namely that running the ball from a spread offense is problematic at best, inherently unimaginative, and incapable of controlling the tempo of the game. "Ball control!" critical coaches cry out, cringing at the thought of an empty backfield. While many coaches have embraced the spread, just as many don't see the point in running an offense that can't control the tempo of the game. These coaches see the spread not as a high-scoring offense, but as a quick-scoring offense. Run the spread, these coaches say, but make sure you have a well-conditioned defense that can play at peak intensity for an entire game.

The challenge, then, is to enable a team to run the typical high-powered spread passing game with an imaginative, aggressive, versatile, and, above all, plausible running attack. This has been done by coupling a spread air-oriented attack with the philosophy of a wishbone offense, which is to use misdirection to confuse a defense and enlarge the number of possible ball-handlers on any given play. In the truest sense, this is the spread: spread the field, spread the formation, spread the amount of touches, and spread the defense. Its proper name is not necessarily the spread, but instead the spread bone or, more whimsically, the Gulf Coast Offense.

Characteristics of the Spread Bone

Those who wish to appropriately and effectively run the spread bone will display an offense with the following four characteristics. Without applying all of these general guidelines to your spread bone offense, you will not achieve the full potential of the package.

Aggressiveness

It's a sure bet that a majority of coaches would rather run the ball than throw it, especially when they aren't gifted with a natural passer at quarterback. When the forward pass came into the rule books, it was regarded with suspicion by coaches who saw no need to gain in the air what they could easily gain on the ground with a straight handoff and a cloud of dust. Even today, with the pass attack dominating the college and professional games, many coaches still approach the forward pass with a certain amount of wariness. It is, after all, a bigger risk than a simple handoff or option pitch.

But the perceived risk may not manifest itself in reality. If you are a coach looking to run the spread with any degree of success, the first thing you must do is cease looking at the forward pass as a high-risk play. This does not mean that you must dedicate your offense to an air-oriented attack. Instead, you must have an aggressive mentality and be able to call whatever play is needed, whether it is a pass play or not. Without the threat of the pass, as in most offenses, the spread is just another set of useless formations. The forward pass, just like a handoff or a pitch, is fundamental to the game of football and must be worked on until the actions are second nature. Whoever said, "Only three things can happen when you throw the football, and two of them are bad," never addressed the parallel equation. Arguably, only three things can happen when you run the football as well, and two of them are bad (a fumble or a loss of yardage).

Practice makes perfect, and the simple truth is that coaches and athletes are so used to seeing, practicing, and performing the fundamentals of the run that they've forgotten its risks. The goal of this book is to enable you to make the same statement about the fundamentals of the passing game. Whether on the air or on the ground, you are going to take risks. Coach your team, practice the fundamentals, and call the best play for the situation, regardless of its orientation. You must think of a pass as just another run, a controlled play to gain a certain desired amount of yardage.

The appropriate aggressive mentality is reflected in a coach who will take what the defense is giving him, regardless of the perceived risk involved. If, for instance, the defense is coming up to stop the run and is giving you the deep ball, an aggressive coach takes the long pass and moves the ball down the field, whether his running game was in complete control or not. Obviously, ball control has its time and place, and situations arise in which it becomes necessary to run the ball and, by extension, the clock. The spread, however, is not a hammer, slamming an opponent into dull submission with brute force. It's a rapier, sharp, slender, and quick. The spread is used to pick a defense apart, inflicting numerous wounds with the rapidity of lightning, taking control from the defense by opening up the entire field to an attack during any one play.

Remember, when you are on offense you are on the attack. Your chosen weapon is the spread, best suited for surgical strikes that bleed your opponent white rather than mash him into a pulp.

Flexibility

One of the basic characteristics of the spread and its spread bone derivative is the inherent flexibility of the offense. The offensive coordinator or head coach must be able to call the exact right play for any given situation. In other words, absolutely no plays can fall outside the team's play-calling system.

Most colleges in the country utilize a number-based passing tree that enables them to call any combination of routes that they need. While the advantage of this flexibility is obvious, some coaches still cling to the older method of tagging a certain combination of routes with a descriptive name (e.g., slam, shoot, or slide). Still others have embraced a number-oriented play-calling system, but have mishandled the passing tree in a way that still limits the number of combinations. Either system, while perfectly acceptable in other offenses, does not give the spread enough flexibility. In effect, you are needlessly limiting what you can do instead of converting to a more pliable play-calling system.

Chapter 2 presents a play-calling system that encompasses every need for flexibility out of the spread, and should serve as a guide to any coach wishing to run the spread bone with the maximum amount of potential.

Misdirection

Many coaches have a natural interest in military history. It's no coincidence that many coaches are involved in teaching history to a younger generation in addition to their duties on the practice field. The correlation between the two studies—history and football—are easily drawn. Both involve the leading of armored men into combat on a field of battle. Even the terms used in football are reminiscent of a more militaristic background, including guard, flanker, sweeps, traps, sneaks, long bombs, and defensive line.

It follows, then, that the strategies involved in a successful military campaign would also serve a football coach on the gridiron. One of the most basic offensive tenets, on the battlefield or the football field, is the use of misdirection. Coaches have been taking advantage of this maneuver since the earliest days of the game. Indeed, almost every offense ever conceived has used misdirection in some way as an integral component. The best example is, of course, the wishbone, an offense that uses a loaded backfield and numerous countermovements and cross flows to confuse the defense. This unique combination of a substantial number of possible ball carriers and the military technique of the feint has not been equaled in the game of football...until now.

The spread has not leant itself well to misdirection in its running game. Many coaches are unable to see how sneaky you can get with only a single runner in the backfield. A simple quarterback counter and a variety of draws can always be found in the typical spread package, but other than that, the misdirection well seemingly has run dry. The common consensus seems to be that the spread is incapable of any truly intricate deception, though if this is true it is only because the imagination of those implementing the spread has been very limited.

The spread needs misdirection. It is the one offense that would benefit most from the deception like that found in the wishbone offense. It helps to think of this issue in military terms: a typical defense has a stout defensive line, defenders on the flanks, and two levels of reserves that can come up to assist, plugging the holes in the defensive front. When facing the spread, the enemy is forced to commit its reserve to the flanks and to the rear, and to widen its defensive line. The enemy is spread, stretched thin, with little to no possibility of immediate support if the offense breaks through the line. In a typical wishbone offense, misdirection helps to scatter the opposing force, which has concentrated its defense in the middle of the field to counter the offensive grouping at the center of the line. The deception helps to spread that defensive cluster and give the offense a chance at a break. With the spread, the defense is already fragmented. Misdirection then achieves a greater effect for a smaller amount of effort. Enter the spread bone, an offense specifically designed to take advantage of what the defense offers when you line up in a one-back set.

Explosiveness

The final characteristic of the spread is actually a derivative of the other three, a natural result of running a proper spread bone. With an aggressive offensive mentality, flexibility, and misdirection, any spread team can be said to have truly explosive offensive potential. The spread, more than any other offense, has the ability to score quickly and often. Leads of four scores or more are not safe from this potent offensive attack. With the use of the spread, the game is truly never over until it's over.

The game itself has been forced to change due to the advent of the spread. Never before were offenses able to score with such speed. Standard ball-control teams have to scramble to come up with some kind of spread equivalent to include in their game plans to ensure that they, too, can strike from behind if need be. Once behind a spread team, ball-control running games have little chance of ever recapturing the lead using their normal offense. The game is changing, with all offenses becoming hybrids, each seeking to incorporate some aspect of the spread passing game to level the playing field.

The spread bone is a child of the necessity to incorporate two offensive philosophies into one coherent whole. While the spread is truly a great offensive weapon, it also is the only defense against an opponent that is running the spread as well. "The only good defense," it has been said, "is a good offense." The only defense against a true spread... is a true spread.

The mentality and characteristics of the spread will be met with scorn and censure in some quarters of the coaching profession. You can easily imagine a critic describing an aggressive mentality as pure recklessness, flexibility as needless complexity, misdirection as useless finesse, and explosive potential as a lack of ball control. And, for certain offenses, those critiques are entirely justified.

However, if you've picked up this book you are obviously intrigued by what the spread has to offer, and it is to such readers and coaches that the philosophy of this chapter is essential. If you are serious about running the spread bone, you must also embrace the given mentality just as seriously. A timid offensive mindset will not lend itself to the spread bone, or any spread offense. A rigid, simplistic, and generalized play-calling system will not give the spread bone the needed flexibility. A playbook of simple counters and draws will not give the spread bone the element of deception that is vital to the confusion of the defense. Finally, a team that does not possess the ability to score quickly in addition to being able to control the tempo will not survive in the game as it's played today. In essence, you have now been given the appropriate mindset to be able to compete in a spread offense. The choice of whether or to adopt that mindset is yours.

The Toolbox

"But my quarterback isn't a great athlete." . . . "None of my receivers will play at the next level." . . . "We aren't big enough up-front." . . . "We don't have a breakaway back."
—Anonymous coaches on running the spread

The same conversation can be heard at any coaching clinic in the country. Two coaches are in a dialogue over the merits, or lack thereof, of the spread offense. Coach #1 is impressed by the offensive numbers put up by Coach #2's spread game plan, but insists that his athletes are incapable of running such an offense.

At this point a perplexed look crosses the face of Coach #2, because if you don't have the athletes to run the spread, then what do you have the athletes to do? After a few seconds of internal deliberation and confusion, Coach #2 finally responds, "You don't have the athletes to do what?" "To throw the ball 50 times a game," replies Coach #1.

Silence falls. Coach #2 starts shaking his head slowly, realizing that each of the coaches is talking about a very different offense. This scenario has played out in countless clinics in countless cities amongst countless coaches. Most coaches simply don't know that the spread is not a "fun-n-gun"-type of air-only attack. Like the first coach in this example, most coaches know very little about the spread offense, either philosophically or practically.

This conversation also illustrates perhaps the most common misconception about the spread offense—the need for great athletes. Fortunately for Coach #1 and every other coach looking to get into an exciting new offense, the spread doesn't require perfect athletes—just perfect execution, a concept based on discipline rather than pure talent.

Great talent is not the cornerstone of a great offense. Hardworking players and competent coaching make for great offense. Every coach in America hopes the next big-time quarterback or Division I prospect running back graces their hallways. Most coaches, however, must work with what they have. In the end, players do not make the offense. They may simplify the process, but they do not make the offense. They execute it. Coaches who use sound fundamental strategy make a great offense.

If versatility is a beautiful thing, then the spread bone offense offers substantial beauty. The ability to attack a defense from multiple angles allows for offensive creativity and explosion. This is a concept that needs to be embraced, first and foremost, by your coaching staff. For the spread bone to work, you must surround yourself with like-minded coaches. This does not mean that everyone must be a lover of the spread. Rather, they should believe in taking what the defense gives you and running (or throwing) with it. The spread bone, as mentioned before, is a philosophy, and like any philosophy it requires discipline, from both the coaches and the athletes.

Discipline can dictate a single drive, a game, or a season. The discipline in question is not "yes sir, no sir" discipline, but rather the discipline to take the five yard hitch, or run the counter until it is stopped. This type of discipline is difficult for some, but it is a must for success. All too often coaches do not have the patience to methodically drive the field, especially when running the vaunted spread offense. A coach must have the patience to take the hitch, and slant, and swing route down the field for six points. A coach must have the patience to understand that the rewards will come, not just on long scoring drives, but in the forthcoming defensive adjustments that will ultimately open up new windows and holes, allowing for offensive versatility. Patience is at the heart of this discipline, and discipline is at the heart of the offense; possession of both will lead to explosive numbers regardless of talent. In the sections to come, you will discover what a coach needs to run the spread bone: the technical details, the type of athletes, and the rest of the specifics involved in forming a basic spread bone playbook. In this chapter, however, you will truly explore the belly of the beast.

Basic Terminology

In this section, and throughout the diagrams given in the rest of this book, abbreviations and symbols will be used to represent the players on any particular play. Most of these symbols and terms are familiar to coaches in general; the spread, however, is a new enough concept to require specific information. The following terms and symbols should give you an absolutely clear picture of the playbook.

Player Symbols

For the remainder of this book, positions will be referred to by the names given to them in Figure 2-1. It is recommended that both coaches and players convert to this naming system (never referring to a tight end as anything other than the Y, or the Y-back, for example) to avoid any potential confusion.

Symbol	Position
X	Split end
Y	Tight end
Z-back	Flanker
H-back	Halfback
A-back	Tailback
QB	Quarterback
LT	Left tackle
LG	Left guard
C	Center
RG	Right guard
RT	Right tackle

Figure 2-1. Player symbols

Before delving any deeper into basic terminology, it's important to have a general picture of the spread bone offense. The base formation, which will be discussed in detail in the next section, is a double slot set—what the spread bone refers to as silver—and incorporates four potential running threats and five potential receivers on any one play. These potential ballcarriers include a sure-handed quarterback, an explosive outside threat at A-back, and two receiver/running back hybrids (the H- and Z-backs) who are equally adept at either catching or running with the football. From this base formation, the spread bone will show an aggressive, flex bone–style ground attack and a wide-open explosive air game in a perfectly balanced offense.

Basic Spread Bone Formations

The formations illustrated here are used in the base spread bone package. The base formation for the spread bone is silver, a double slot set with two wide split ends. Formations are referred to not by popular names, but as colors, an extremely simple system for athletes to grasp and take as their own. Within the spread bone offense the Y always goes to the strength call and, unless otherwise specified, always lines up on the line of scrimmage. Receiver alignment differs in each offensive formation, though simplicity is always strived for. The following examples are all right sets, thus placing the Y on the right side of the formation.

Silver (Figure 2-2)

Silver is a double slot set. The Z-back and H-back both line up one yard deep and one yard wide in a slot. The X and Y receivers are lined up at the top of the numbers and on the line of scrimmage. The A-back is five yards deeper than the quarterback's ankles, lined up directly over center. This is the spread bone's base formation.

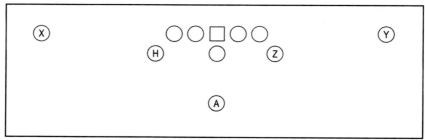

Figure 2-2. Silver

Black (Figure 2-3)

Black is a true doubles set. The Y is the split end at the top of the numbers, and the Z-back is splitting the difference between the Y and the right tackle. The H-back mirrors the Z-back on the opposite side of the ball. The X and Y are on the line, while the H-back and Z-back are off the line. The A-back is five yards deeper than the quarterback's ankles, lined up directly over center.

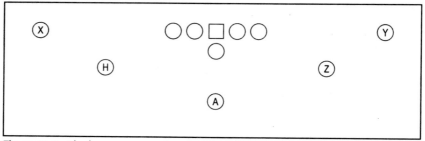

Figure 2-3. Black

Black Slot (Figure 2-4)

Black slot is a doubles set with a weakside slot. The H-back lines up one yard away from the left tackle and one yard deep in the backfield, in a standard slot position. The Y still remains on the line of scrimmage while the Z-back stays off. No change takes place in the backfield.

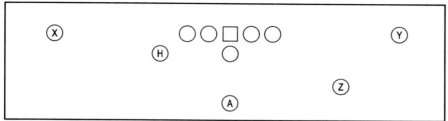

Figure 2-4. Black slot

Blue (Figure 2-5)

Blue is a tight end set with twins split to the weakside. The X and Z-back are at the top of the numbers. The H-back splits the difference between the left tackle and the X. The Y comes into a true tight-end set, following typical lineman split rules—4-feet between the Y and the right tackle.

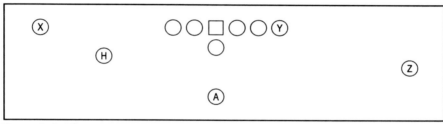

Figure 2-5. Blue

Blue Slot (Figure 2-6)

Similar to blue, blue slot places the H-back and Z-back in a slot position. Their alignment in this set is the same as in silver—one-yard split from the left tackle and one-yard deep in the backfield. This is primarily a power-running formation for short-yardage or goal-line situations.

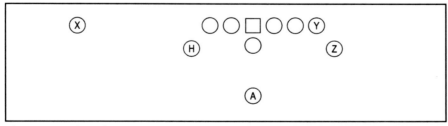

Figure 2-6. Blue slot

Red (Figure 2-7)

Red is a trips set with a strongside tight end. The H-back splits the difference between the Z-back and the Y, and lines up off the line of scrimmage.

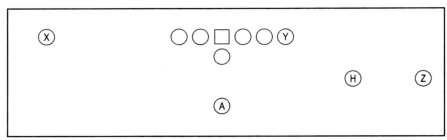

Figure 2-7. Red

Red Wing (Figure 2-8)

Similar to the red formation, red wing puts the H-back in a wing. His alignment should be one yard wide of the Y and one yard off the ball. The X and Z-back are at the top of the numbers, with the Z-back remaining off the line of scrimmage.

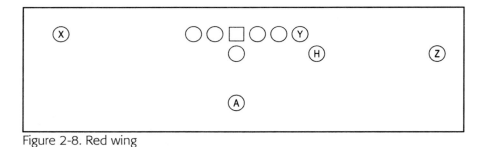

Figure 2-8. Red wing

Gold (Figure 2-9)

Gold is a standard trips set. The X and Z-back line up at the top of the numbers. The trips receivers (H-back, Y, and Z-back) need to have a six-yard split between each other.

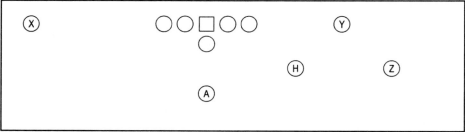

Figure 2-9. Gold

Gold Bunch (Figure 2-10)

Gold bunch is also a standard trips set, similar to the gold formation, with the H-back, Y, and Z-back receivers in a bunch set. The bunch needs to shift its alignment inside until the H-back is approximately five yards wider than the right tackle. The X remains lined up at the top of the numbers.

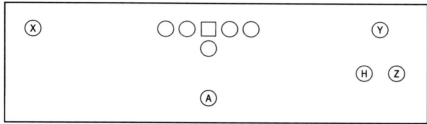

Figure 2-10. Gold bunch

Gold Tight (Figure 2-11)

Gold tight is a trips set, similar to the gold bunch formation, with the H-back, Y, and Z-back receivers in a bunch set. The bunch needs to shift its alignment inside until the H-back is approximately one yard wider than the right tackle. The X remains lined up at the top of the numbers.

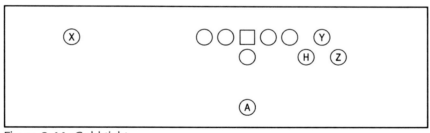

Figure 2-11. Gold tight

Grey (Figure 2-12)

Grey is sometimes referred to as an ace, or double tight, set, with two true tight ends and two split ends. The X and Z-back are off the line of scrimmage and are lined up at the top of the numbers.

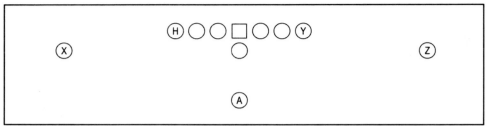

Figure 2-12. Grey

Tiger (Figure 2-13)

Tiger is sometimes called an empty, spread, or five-wide set. The Z-back lines up at the top of the numbers and off the ball. The A-back goes into the slot position with the Y playing on the line of scrimmage and one yard wide of the A-back. The H-back is in the slot position away from the call with the X at the top of the numbers.

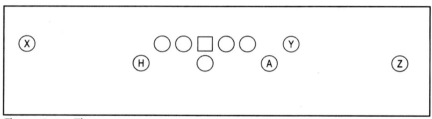

Figure 2-13. Tiger

The Passing Tree

The ability to adapt week to week with little change in terminology or specific play names is a necessity in any spread offense. The following passing tree outlines 10 playside routes as well as the rules and routes for backside receivers. The use of this tree will be explained in detail in the play-calling section later in this chapter.

Frontside Routes

0—*Hitch*: The receiver begins with his inside foot forward. He drives as hard as he can upfield for three steps. On the third step, he punches and pivots to meet the ball.

1—*Quick slant*: The receiver begins with his inside foot forward and drives upfield for three steps. On the fourth step, he plants at a 45-degree angle and accelerates on a path toward the goal post. The depth of the route can vary week-to-week, depending upon linebacker coverage. The first three steps of the hitch and slant should look the same to a defender.

2—*Shoot*: This is a three-step route. The receiver begins with his inside foot forward and drives upfield for two steps. Then he takes a 45-degree angle on his third step, angling toward the sideline. He begins to flatten out his route on his fourth step.

3—*Dig*: The receiver begins with his inside foot forward and drives 10 to 12 yards upfield. The receiver then breaks across the middle of the field. If the receiver recognizes man coverage he will continue across the formation. If the receiver reads zone coverage he will look for a window, an opening in the coverage, to settle into.

4—*Out*: The receiver begins with his inside foot forward and drives 13 to 14 yards upfield. The receiver then plants and comes back downfield to 10 to 12 yards. It is important that the receiver comes back to meet the ball.

5—*Post/curl*: The receiver begins with his inside foot forward and drives 10 yards upfield before breaking off at a 45-degree angle toward the goal post. If the safety is in his backpedal or is playing "soft," then the receiver will break off the route at 15 yards and bring it back down to 12 yards. If the safety is playing tight or "hard," then the receiver will continue on his original route and attack the deep middle of the field in a standard post route.

6—*Flag*: The receiver begins with his inside foot forward and pushes 10 to 12 yards upfield. He then makes a 45-degree cut toward the sideline. The receiver wants to run his route in between the safety and the cornerback; therefore, the depth of the route will vary depending upon coverage.

7—*Rail/beam*: The receiver begins with his inside foot forward and drives upfield for three steps. On the fourth step, he starts to bend his route toward the sideline (the rail) or toward the middle of the field (the beam). Once clear of the covering defender, the receiver straightens his route out and finishes the play by fading toward the sideline or the middle of the field, depending upon the desired route.

8—*Arrow*: The receiver begins with his inside foot forward and attacks inside at a 45-degree angle for four hard steps. He then "whips," or throws his inside shoulder to the side of the field, forcing him to open up and push back toward the sideline at about a five yard depth.

9—*Go*: The receiver begins with his inside foot forward and drives upfield running just inside the numbers, allowing the quarterback to place the ball on his outside shoulder, thereby bending the receiver into the sideline. This route can also vary depending upon coverage, changing into a seam-type route rather than a fade.

Backside Routes

The simplicity of the spread bone passing offense lies in the rules applying to backside receivers. With few exceptions, the routes are always the same, and are designed to perfectly complement any combination of playside routes.

The receiver farthest from the ball will always run a skinny post. The second receiver will run a dig route, sometimes called a "search" route; the receiver's goal is to find a window and give the quarterback a clear passing lane (Figure 2-14).

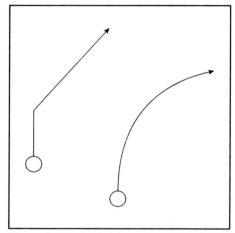

Figure 2-14. Backside routes

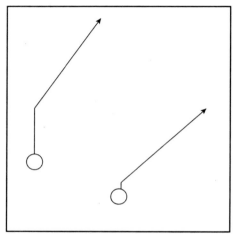

Figure 2-15. Alternate backside routes

These rules only change when a dig or beam route is called on the frontside. In this situation, the receiver who would run a backside dig now runs a shallow cross at a depth of four yards (Figure 2-15). This combination gives a traditional cross look and prevents the two routes from running into each other.

Some coaching points to keep in mind involve the dig route and the skinny post. The dig route is intended to find the "soft" spot in the zone coverage. Typically, the receiver will settle at about 12 yards in the middle of the field. The skinny post is used to pull backside corners and safeties in an attempt to create single-coverage situations or create seams for frontside crossing routes.

Play-Calling System

The spread bone utilizes a play-calling system that allows for the maximum amount of flexibility, while remaining inherently simple. A designated sequence is used when calling plays (Figure 2-16).

Sequence	Example
1. Strength	Right
2. Formation (including "Gun" call)	Right black gun
3. A-back alignment	Right black gun liz
4. Motion	Right black gun liz Z-thru
5. Play (including play tag)	Right black gun liz Z-thru 146
6. Tagged route (speaks to third receiver in route)	Right black gun liz Z-thru 146 go

Figure 2-16. Play-calling sequence

On the face of it, right black gun liz Z-thru 146 go is a mouthful, a horrendous complexity that high school athletes will never be able to grasp. In reality, this is the most complicated play that can be called in this system, and an athlete only needs to focus on a small part of each play call. For example, for this play, the H-back only needs to know how to run right black 146 go.

This system also uses an abbreviated "code," usually only one or two letters, that indicates line blocking and play-type simultaneously. In the spread bone, a "G" refers to any play using a guard pull (mostly traps and powers). Likewise, a "GT" refers to a play utilizing a guard and tackle pull (almost always counters). "O" refers to option blocking, and the term "zone" refers to full zone blocking by the offensive line. Other combinations exist (like "GTO"), but they all build off of the four basic play-tags.

Play-call numbers ranging from 80 to 800 are used in the spread bone passing series; anything lower is a running play. The first number will always refer to the strength. Even first numbers are plays run to the strongside of the call and odd first numbers are plays run to the weakside of the call.

The 80/90 series refers to all passes that originate with a three-step drop by the quarterback; these passes are usually meant to be quick and sharp. The spread bone uses the 100/200 plays as its deep-drop series; a half-roll drop is used in place of a typical five-step quarterback drop. Instead, the quarterback will roll back and set up behind the playside guard. This series is used for pass plays that need some time to develop.

The spread bone passing game is rounded out by the 300/400 series (sprint-out passes), the 500/600 series (bootleg and waggle passes), and the 700/800 series, which includes the offense's screen game.

Running Series

The ground attack out of the spread bone is designated by a two numeral play call and an abbreviated play tag. The first number refers to the player who will actually wind up carrying the football and can be any number from a one to a four (one referencing the quarterback, two the Z-back, three the H-back, and four the A-back). The point of attack is designated by the second number in the play call, using the basic hole numbers used by most offenses (Figure 2-17).

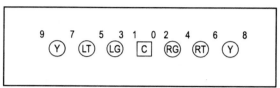

Figure 2-17. Basic numbering of holes

Calling a Running Play in the Spread Bone: Three Examples

☐ 45 G: Remember, the first number refers to the person who will receive the ball from the quarterback. The second number refers to the target hole. The third part of the call tags the type of play and speaks primarily to the linemen, varying their blocking scheme. In a 45 G, the A-back is taking the ball and attacking the 5-hole, with the linemen blocking the power with a G block (Figure 2-18).

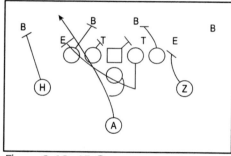

Figure 2-18. 45 G

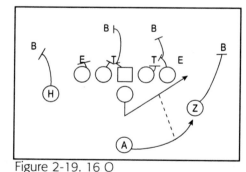

Figure 2-19. 16 O

☐ 16 O: This play entails the quarterback attacking the 6-hole, running a speed option (Figure 2-19).

☐ 30 G: This play involves the H back running through the 0-hole, with trap blocking (Figure 2-20).

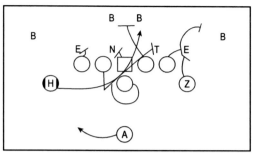

Figure 2-20. 30 G

Passing Series

Calling a Passing Play in the Spread Bone: Two Examples

Remember, the first number is the passing series indicator, the second number tells the outside receiver his route, and the third number tells the inside receiver his route. Backside receivers run the standard backside routes. When three possible playside receivers exist, the third receiver runs a designated route (e.g., 175 hitch). The A-back is never kept in to block unless in a blitz pickup situation. Instead, he always fades into the flat (usually to the playside) as a safety valve unless another route is designated (for example, in 175 hitch, the A-back runs a hitch route).

☐ Right silver 80: This example shows that all receivers run a 0 route or a hitch. Because the call was right 80 the quarterback looks to the right side of the formation.

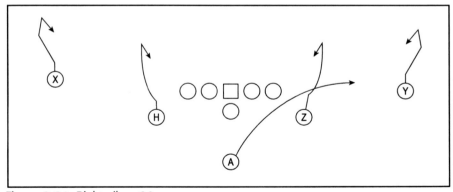

Figure 2-21. Right silver 80

☐ Right black rip H-thru 238 flag: On this play, the Y runs an 8 route, the Z-back runs a 3 route, and the H-back runs a flag route. The quarterback does a half-roll to the strength call, or to the right. In other words, 200 series passes are thrown to strength.

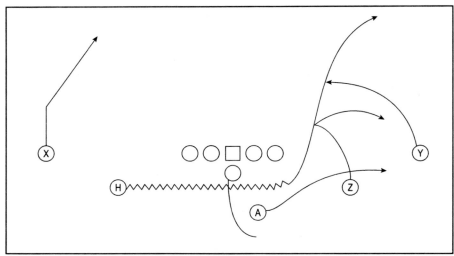

Figure 2-22. Right black rip H-thru 238 flag

Labeling and Using Motion

Three types of motion are used: thru, away, and in. To call the motion, simply state the desired player and then the motion required. For example, calling an H-thru tells the H-back to run a thru motion. The desired stopping point for any given motion is to be determined by the coach based on the design of the play.

- Thru motion: This motion takes place when any player begins on one side of the ball and motions through the ball.
- Away motion: This motion happens when a player begins in a slot or in the backfield and is motioned away from the ball without crossing it.
- In motion: This motion occurs when a player begins in a slot, wing, or wide-out position and is motioned into the backfield.

It's important to note that when using motion in the passing game, if a receiver is motioned to trips he becomes the third playside receiver and must now run the tagged route. For example, in right black Z thru 175 hitch the Z-back runs the tagged route, the hitch, because he is the receiver motioning into the trips.

A-back Alignment

Three basic alignments are available to the A-back, two of which can be called on any given play. His normal alignment is five yards behind the quarterback's ankles, directly behind the center in a two-point stance. In a rip or liz set, the A-back is offset and lines up either behind the right guard (rip) or the left guard (liz). These sets are used both when the quarterback is under center and in the shotgun. Offsetting the back can be helpful in deceiving a defense in the running and passing game.

A-back Involvement in the Passing Game

The A-back is a critical part of the dropback-passing game. The rules for the A-back in the dropback-passing game are as follows:

- Run a shoot route to the strength call.
- In red or gold, run the shoot route away from the strength.

The A-back's responsibilities in the sprint-out series are slightly different. The A-back rules for the sprint series are:

- Capture and protect the pocket's edge (cutting outside threats).
- If the edge is protected, release into the flats on a shoot route.

The A-back also has some blitz pickup responsibilities that are outlined in the next section.

Offensive Line Play

A spread bone offensive line is, ideally, a quick and mean group of individuals. The guards play in a two-point stance to maximize their speed and their ability to pull with utmost power and quickness, while the two tackles remain in three-point stances to retain their strength and leverage. The line splits are wider than average—four-foot splits force the defense to either weaken its front line by widening in response or take a chance on giving up the quick outside run by stacking the defense. The following rules apply to the designated play series.

100/200 Series (The Five-step Series)

Guards and Tackles

At the snap of the ball, the linemen want to take one step out and one step back, punching with both hands and maintaining arms-length separation between themselves and the defensive linemen. Once the defensive lineman has engaged the offensive player, he will then take the defensive player where he wants to go, preferably wide to the outside. This is designed to create a flexible pocket for the quarterback to work in.

Center

At the snap of the ball, the center will take one step straight back and look to protect the A gaps to either side of him. If the guards are handling their assignments, and the linebackers are not threatening the A gap with a delayed blitz, the center can look to the edge.

His assignment at that time is to fly to the endangered edge and cut the oncoming threat with extreme prejudice. If the center is covered at the snap of the ball, or his A gaps are threatened, he will engage and steer the defensive man to either side, creating a natural throwing lane.

This basic line play is commonly called "Big on Big," or BOB, blocking, the offensive line equivalent of man coverage. Before the snap of the ball, linemen must communicate and verbally tag the man they are responsible for blocking. Rarely will there be a play without some sort of defensive stunt, most likely a twist-type blitz that threatens to overwhelm the center by charging both A gaps. Any potential stunt involving both A gaps should result in a "help" call from the center. A "help" call automatically splits A gap responsibility between two individuals, the center and the A back, and overrides the A back's normal pass responsibility. With a "help" call, the center takes the on-the-line threat and the A back the linebacker threat (in the case of a defensive tackle/inside linebacker stunt). In the case of a stunt involving both inside linebackers shooting the A gaps, the center takes the playside backer while the A back takes the backside defender.

As more and more defenses adopt a 3-3 stack look to counter the spread offense, it's wise to anticipate seeing such a defense and having a handy pass-protection adjustment. Upon recognizing a 3-3 stack, the center will issue an "area" call (Figure 2-23). In this case, blocking responsibility is assigned in pairs—the playside guard and tackle are responsible for the strongside defensive end and his stacked linebacker; likewise, the offside guard and tackle must block the weakside defensive end and his respective backer. This leaves the center and the A-back to pair off on the noseguard and the inside linebacker. It's best left to the quickest three (both guards and the A-back) to take their pair's assigned linebackers, which leaves the center and both tackles to handle the defensive linemen.

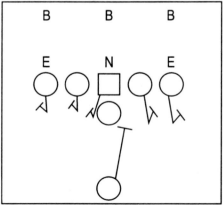
Figure 2-23. Area call

In the case of any overloaded or uncovered outside threat, the quarterback can call for "pro" blocking. In other words, he will call for the backside flex or slot receiver to motion into a true slot and pick up the outside threat on the endangered edge.

Should a lineman other than the center find himself uncovered, he should know that the center has been taken out of the blocking equation in an unexpected way, usually due to a defensive stunt, and the uncovered lineman must now assume the center's assignment—namely, to proceed to the endangered edge and cut the rush.

300/400 Series (The Sprint-Out Series)

For the sprint-out series, all five linemen follow the gate principles, meaning that they will "step and hinge," taking one step wide and one step back, while looking to turn their backside to the sprint-out call, eventually having their back to the quarterback. This action will create a natural "gate" between the quarterback and the defensive linemen.

500/600 Series (The Boot/Waggle Series) and 700/800 Series (The Screen Series)

Offensive line play will vary according to each play. See Chapter 3 for examples and explanations of assignments.

What Kind of Athletes Are Needed?

Remember, great athletes are not a necessity (though, as any coach will tell you, they certainly are welcome!). However, certain positions require athletes with specific skills, and it's these skills that you must ingrain in those who seek to play these positions. This section focuses on the four most demanding positions on the field for those running a spread bone: the quarterback, the H-back/Z-back, the A-back, and the center, as well as a special note on the offensive line.

The Quarterback

A trend is currently underway in football that says you need a star at quarterback. Perhaps some validity is behind to this trend. However, within the spread bone offense, a quarterback who can be a good all-around athlete is truly what is needed.

The quarterback position requires great discipline and understanding, as the quarterback is required to make presnap and live-play reads. Therefore, field awareness is a must. However, this is not just a stand-and-throw offense. The quarterback must have the ability to run when necessary. Also, a high level of ambidexterity is needed as the option and shovel pitches play a substantial role in the spread bone offense. All in all, your quarterback must be your best ballhandler.

The H-back/Z-back

This position is the most complicated one on the field. The H-back/Z-back position demands a player with size and speed who can run, block and catch. This is your fullback or wingback type of player—a ballcarrier who can catch when needed. Ideally, this is a player who has the ability to carry the ball 10 to 15 times a game and contribute to the passing game in a substantial way. More importantly, they need to want to carry the ball, because in the spread bone offense they're going to get the ball a lot.

The A-back

In a spread offense, everyone must be able to catch the ball. No exception is made for backs, as they are consistently included in the passing game. In addition, the A-back must be a capable ballcarrier. In fact, this is the position often referred to as a tailback, or the primary ballcarrier. If the H-back is the bruiser back, the A-back is your slasher—quicker, leaner, and more explosive in the open field.

The Center

Without a doubt, the most difficult position on the field to play is center. The center must have the on-field knowledge of a quarterback and the feet of a linebacker. Contrary to popular thought, the center must be your best lineman—able to move, block, think on his feet, and show extreme aggression. If the quarterback is the on-field general, then the center is the colonel, responsible for the play of the offensive line as a whole. The center will consistently be asked to make calls at the line, pull, and work backside on blitz pick-ups.

Offensive Line

A special note is required regarding the type of linemen needed for the spread bone. Little argument takes place between coaches regarding the key to offensive power. The offensive linemen and their subsequent play will dictate the success of your offense. Gone are the days of the 300-pound threat to the buffet line. The spread bone offense is not in the business of brute force, but rather of quick, aggressive line play. The spread bone lineman must be smaller, quicker, and twice as mean as their larger counterparts.

In Defense of Taking the Snap Under Center

The current vogue in the spread game is to take the snap from center exclusively from the shotgun formation. While the shotgun definitely has its place in any spread game plan (see Chapter 5 for a dedicated spread bone running game), taking the snap from under center is strongly advocated. The reason is, simply, that the shotgun deprives the quarterback of a precious half-second immediately following the snap during which he has to glance down at the oncoming football. This takes his eyes off his presnap reads, whether for the pass or for the run, during the exact time he needs to be scanning the field and making his initial pass decisions.

3

The Running Game

"Ut Falles Vincesque"

—Latin, "To Deceive and Conquer"

The Holy Grail for most spread coaches is the ever-elusive successful running attack. The most popular way to balance out the potency of the spread air attack has been to utilize the spread formations to run a powerful option-oriented ground game, and rightly so. The option attack relies on the high-speed, high-stress, element of the game itself to force the defense to make mistakes. Using the triple option is a good approach, but not one this book will champion. The spread bone, while still incorporating elements of an option attack, does not rely on it as its bread-and-butter play. The spread bone uses a flex bone–type ground attack to deceive and exploit an entire fresh defense rather than make one tired, stressed, and confused defender make a mistake. Additionally, the spread bone has no need to revert to an unfamiliar, uncharacteristic, and unsuitable power-run formation on short yardage or goal line situations, a fallacy of typical spread option–type teams. While there remains a time and a place for a loaded, power-run type of formation, the spread bone does not need to use it to run the ball successfully for short yardage.

Many of the plays covered in this chapter purposefully employ similar back paths and movements, the goal being to make the defense commit to every possible play angle. As this book is organized according to series (10s/20s/30s/40s/specials), each play description includes a list of related plays—in other words, plays with related back movement. The related plays are also given a specific "set" name for simplicity. For example, the first play discussed in the 10 Series, the 10/11 G, is part of the alpha set.

For simplicity's sake, all plays are shown out of the base formation, silver, against a split-type defense, unless back movement between different formations is entirely dissimilar, in which case a variety of diagrams will be shown. In addition, the 20/30 series are shown together, given that they are exactly the same in line play and back movement. The only difference, of course, is that in one series the H-back is the ball handler, and in the other the Z-back is the ball handler.

The playbook given in these pages, passing game included, are only intended as the basis for a successful spread bone attack. The object is to give coaches the very base plays of a spread bone offense, and to that end the most basic four or five plays in each series are diagramed and shown. Obviously certain defensive alignments and situations will arise that this book does not cover. Again, this book is not intended for amateurs, but for professional coaches who need some help in implementing the spread bone offense.

The 10 Series: The Quarterback

10/11 G

☐ Related Plays
The alpha set:
• 48/49 G-zone
• 30/31 G
• 30/31 G.O.
• 20/21 G
• 20/21 G.O.

The quarterback trap is the base in the alpha set, the first in a series of plays with similar back paths and line blocking (Figure 3-1). On the snap of the ball, the quarterback reverses out and fakes a pitch to the A-back, who has taken a definite counter step and then proceeded on a hard power sweep path away from the call. He proceeds to throw up his hands as if he's received the quarterback's pitch, and should continue around the offside end as if he's running a true sweep. Remember, this offense is based on deception, and so it's vital that every member of the backfield sells his particular fake—no half measures are allowed. The quarterback, upon completion of his pitch fake, will continue his reversal, tucking away the football and following the trap block of his offside guard up the middle of the field, eventually making his cut decisions based on the play of the linebackers and the approaching safety.

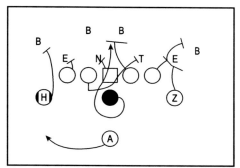

Figure 3-1. Right silver rip 10 G

The blocking of the remaining backs and receivers is quite simple and designed to prevent outside help from reaching the inside trap. The H/Z-backs, in the alpha set, are the trap runners and have two responsibilities. The playside back, in this case the Z-back, collapses down and helps the playside tackle's block on the outside threat on the defensive line, usually the end. The offside back, in this case the H-back, takes one counter step on his trap path toward the center of the line, then balloons out and seeks to prevent the nearest second level linebacker, usually the outside backer, from reaching the inside trap. Receivers, meanwhile, should seek to run their defenders down the field, stalk-blocking them to the outside when the defenders react to the run.

Line play follows normal trap blocking procedure. On 10 G, the left tackle blocks the defensive end out and away from the inside trap. The left guard pulls and traps the playside defensive tackle, driving him out and away from the line of scrimmage. The playside of the line blocks down as a rule—the center on the nose or offside defensive tackle, the right guard will remain locked up on the defensive end, and the right tackle on the linebackers. This last block is the hardest to make. A decision must be made regarding who is the greater threat, the playside or outside backer. The quarterback should be prepared to look first at the result of this block to make his cut decisions.

Though unusual, the blocking scheme advocated for the trap in this book is based on the need to protect the slot back trap from a crashing defensive end. This scheme is drawn up in the following pages for all traps. A more conventional approach would be to release both the playside guard and tackle on the linebackers, and "chip" the defensive end with the playside slot back. The quarterback trap cannot be run out of the shotgun formation, but can be run with little adjustment by most of the formations that include at least one slot back, or involve a movement of a receiver into a slot position through presnap motion. In situations with one slot back, for instance, in black, the slot back performs the duties of the trap runner (hard step towards the trap, then out to block the backside outside backer). With the addition of a true tight end, the Y becomes responsible for blocking the playside defensive end, with the playside slot (if there is one) responsible for the playside outside backer. Variations on this play are shown in Figures 3-2 and 3-3.

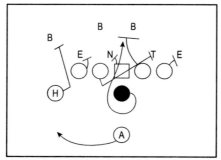

Figure 3-2. Right black slot 10 G

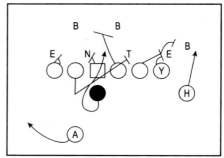

Figure 3-3. Right red wing liz 10 G

Ronald Martinez/Getty Images

The quarterback trap can be run with little adjustment by most of the formations that include at least one slot back, or involve a movement of a receiver into a slot position through presnap motion.

12/13 O: Option

Most flex bone/wishbone-oriented teams run the triple option as their base play, and with good reason. The triple option, as its name suggests, is three powerful plays in one package, three separate attack points your opponent has to defend. Some programs, like the Air Force Academy, have gained notoriety by perfecting the triple option as the cornerstone of their game plan. Obviously the spread bone, as a variant of the flex bone, is well suited to the triple-option attack. The only negative aspect of the triple option out of the spread bone is the need for a presnap slot back "in" motion; the defense will be able to get a split-second key regarding the direction of the play. Regardless, the defense will still have to defend the three-pronged attack of the triple option, and an offensive coordinator can use a lot of "in" motion throughout the game to mask the presence of an upcoming triple option.

Prior to the snap, the quarterback will send the backside slot back, the H-back, into the deep backfield with the "in" motion (Figure 3-4). The quarterback only waits a half-count before calling for the snap; he doesn't wait for the H-back to reach the backfield. On taking the snap, he opens up to the playside, his eyes on his dive read, the playside defensive tackle. At the same time, the A-back has charged up toward the 2-hole, preparing to take the dive handoff. The quarterback rides the handoff, watching the defensive tackle. If the defensive tackle charges the mesh point, the quarterback pulls the ball. If not, the quarterback gives the ball to the A-back. At this point the quarterback has to make a second read. The quarterback may be attacked by the defensive end, in which case flips the ball back and out to the H-back. If he's not attacked, he keeps the ball and cuts up inside the defensive end.

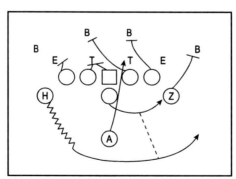

Figure 3-4. Right silver 12 O

Playside line blocking is simple. Regardless of alignment, the playside tackle and guard are responsible for the inside linebackers, leaving the defensive tackle and defensive ends alone as reads. The playside slot back, the Z-back, releases outside to block the outside linebacker. The offside linemen, including the center, are left to zone block to the offside.

14/15 G

> □ Related Plays
> 44/45 G

The power is one of the spread bone's bread-and-butter plays, a power play designed to exploit the explosive potential of your quarterback or A-back to get a quick four or five yards. It's also one of football's oldest schemes, the staple of any power running team. As the old saying goes, if it isn't broke, don't fix it.

As with most plays, the quarterback, on the snap, will reverse out, dropping to a depth of two yards behind the line of scrimmage, immediately tucking the ball away (Figure 3-5). The A-back, without hesitation or counter step, charges hard at the playside tackle (on 15 G, the 5-hole), leading up through the hole. Once through the line of scrimmage, the A-back is the seal block, turning inside to block the nearest threat at the second level (usually the inside linebacker). The quarterback will find his blocker and follow closely on his heels, looking to slash through the second level between the playside linebacker and the playside outside backer.

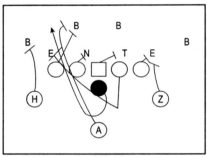

Figure 3-5. Right silver 15 G

That playside outside backer is the blocking responsibility of the playside slot, in this case the H-back, who should endeavor to turn his man out and drive him to the sidelines. The offside slot, the Z-back, drops down to the line of scrimmage to replace the offside tackle, and is responsible for blocking the last man on the defensive line, usually the end. Receivers should seek to run their defenders down the field, stalk-blocking them to the outside when the defenders react to the run.

The power blocking scheme is simple when it comes to the offensive line. The only pull involved is the offside guard, the right guard, who kicks out the end man on the line of scrimmage to the playside, usually the defensive end. All other linemen, with the exception of the backside tackle, the right tackle, zone block down. The playside tackle, the left tackle, seeks to block the second level inside backer, with the left guard and the center blocking down on the defensive tackles.

The quarterback power is a versatile play that can be run out of any one-back formation, and works well out of the gun. Line adjustments are only necessary when no offside slot is available to block the backside defensive end. In that case, the offside tackle blocks the offside defensive end. With the addition of a true tight end, the Y becomes responsible for blocking the playside outside linebacker, with the playside slot (if there is one) responsible for the playside outside backer. Variations can be found in Figure 3-6.

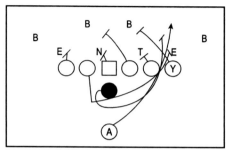

Figure 3-6. Right red 14 G

16/17 O

The speed option has been run out of the spread almost since the spread first came into common use. It's an intuitive play to run out of any one-back, wide-open set. The blocking scheme is simple, the attack aggressive, and the potential outcome enormous.

The most important aspect, of course, is the timing of the option, or the ability to make a quick read and a sure pitch within scant seconds of the snap of the ball.

The speed option is also extremely straightforward. The quarterback takes the snap and opens up to the playside, squaring his shoulders to the sidelines (Figure 3-7). He then charges the line of scrimmage, attacking his read, the inside shoulder of the playside defensive end. The A-back attacks the line of scrimmage at a similar angle, maintaining a five yard pitch relationship with the quarterback. The decision to pitch or to keep the football lies completely in the hands of the quarterback.

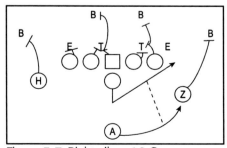

Figure 3-7. Right silver 16 O

Obviously, the playside defensive end has been left unblocked to get an option read. The playside linemen, including the center, block down, with either the right tackle or the right guard looking to reach the second level and block the playside inside linebacker. The playside slot, in this case the Z-back, releases to the outside to block the corresponding outside backer or first outside threat. The backside linemen, the left guard and left tackle, base block on the man over them, in this case the left guard releasing to the second level backer and the left tackle blocking the backside defensive end. The remaining man, the backside slot, in this case the H-back, is responsible for blocking the backside outside backer. Receivers should seek to run their defenders down the field, stalk-blocking them to the outside when the defenders react to the run. The speed option works just as well out of the shotgun, the only adjustment being the A-back's need to maintain proper pitch relationship. Variations on this play are shown in Figures 3-8 through 3-10.

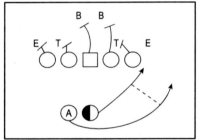

Figure 3-8. Left black liz gun 16 O

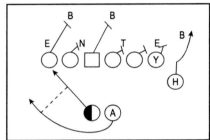

Figure 3-9. Right red wing rip gun 17 O

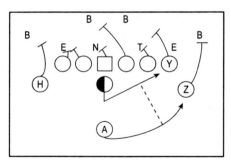

Figure 3-10. Left blue slot 16 O

18/19 O

A natural, but oft-ignored, offshoot of the option running game is the underneath, or shovel, option (Figure 3-11). It's easy to see why this potential play is ignored, as it requires the acquisition of a new type of timing and a new type of quarterback read response. Additionally, instead of sending the ball out and back to an awaiting ball carrier (sending it, in other words, out of the immediate danger of the line of scrimmage), the shovel option attempts to exploit a charging end and consign an option pitch forward into the maelstrom of the defensive line. Set against these negative aspects is the positive gains the shovel option offers, including the possibility of getting the football to a ballhandler while he is at full speed, already with positive forward yardage, with every chance of making a clean break through the second level of the defense. When worked in conjunction with the normal spread option game, the shovel option is a devastating threat to any defense.

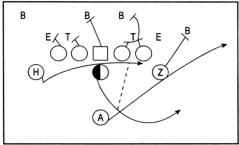

Figure 3-11. Right silver 18 O

The quarterback's path upon receiving the snap emulates that of a sprint-out pass. The quarterback rolls out and starts to slow his sprint-out behind his playside tackle (in other words, he begins to look as if he has found a downfield receiver and is setting up to throw). At the same time, the offside slot back, in this case the H-back, comes all the way across the formation, hugging the backs of his linemen as much as possible, looking back toward the quarterback. The quarterback's read, just like on a normal option play, is the playside defensive end. If he charges the quarterback in the pocket, the quarterback is to shovel-pitch the football to the H-back. Should the defensive end remain on the line of scrimmage, the quarterback takes the ball around the playside end, reading the block of his playside slot back, in this case the Z-back, who has moved downfield to block the outside linebacker.

It's important to make the quarterback's designated path especially clear. His steps are deep into the pocket, enticing the playside defensive end up the field. This is a trap in the strongest sense of the word, playing on any defender's natural aggressive impulse upon seeing the quarterback, his natural prey, unprotected and alone. This play is a designed lure, its target the playside defensive end and its goal being to open up a natural crease in the line.

Line play and blocking are very similar to the blocking found in the speed option, with the exception of the A-back. His path is directly at the playside guard's outside shoulder, his assignment to run a shallow shoot route, never crossing the line of scrimmage. He functions, in the shovel option, as a safety outlet—a dump screen if necessary. The playside defensive end has been left unblocked to get an option read. The playside linemen, including the center, block down, with the right tackle or right guard looking to reach the second level and block the playside inside backer. The playside slot, in this case the Z-back, releases to the outside to block the corresponding outside backer, or first outside threat. The backside linemen, the left guard and left tackle, base block on the man over them. Receivers should seek to run their defenders down the field, stalk-blocking them to the outside when the defenders react to the run, or, in the case of the playside receiver, immediately blocking the corner to the outside. Variations on this play are shown in Figures 3-12 and 3-13.

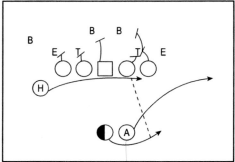

Figure 3-12. Right black slot rip gun 18 O

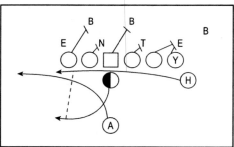

Figure 3-13. Right red wing 19 O

The 20/30 Series: The Z-back/H-back

20/21 and 30/31 G

☐ Related Plays
  The alpha set:
   • 48/49 G-zone
   • 30/31 G.O.
   • 10/11 G
   • 20/21 G.O.

The 20/21 and 30/31 G are obvious offshoots of the 10/11 G, utilizing the same basic back movements and line play as the rest of the alpha set. In a given double slot formation, like silver, two plays are possible: one to the H-back and one to the Z-back. For example, in right silver, the two possible plays are 30 and 21 trap—two backs, two different directions. For the duration of this book, the 20/30 series plays will be represented in the text by the 30 series, with additional diagrams illustrating the 20 series variants.

In 30 G out of a right set, the quarterback reverses out at the snap and fakes a pitch to the A-back, who has taken a hard counter step and then proceeded on a power sweep path away from the call (Figure 3-14). He proceeds to throw up his hands as if he's received the quarterback's pitch, and should continue around the offside end, truly selling the fake. The quarterback, his pitch fake complete, should finish his reversal and give the football to the approaching H-back, who has cut across the formation following the trap block of his offside guard up the middle of the field, eventually making his cut decisions based on the play of the linebackers and the approaching safety.

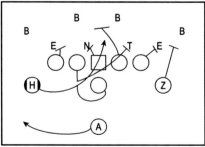

Figure 3-14. Right silver 30 G

The blocking of the remaining backs and receivers remains the same as in the quarterback trap illustrated in the 10 Series section of this chapter. The playside back, in this case the Z-back, collapses down and will help the playside tackle will the defensive end. Receivers, as usual, should seek to run their defenders down the field, stalk-blocking them to the outside when the defenders react to the run.

Line play also remains startling similar to 10 G. The left guard pulls and blocks the playside defensive tackle, while the left tackle blocks the defensive end out and away from the inside trap. The playside of the line blocks down, and the playside guard is once again forced to choose who to block on the second level. Usually the hard sweep motion of the A-back will cause both backers to flow hard to the backside, resulting in the playside backer being in a perfect position to be blocked by the guard. The 20/21 and 30/31 G can be run with little adjustment by most of the formations that include at least one slot back or involve movement of a receiver into a slot position through presnap motion (Figures 3-15 and 3-16).

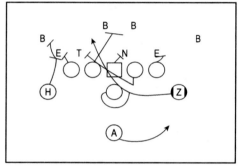

Figure 3-15. Right silver 21 G

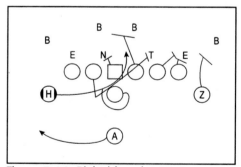

Figure 3-16. Right blue slot 30 G

48

20/21 and 30/31 G.O.

☐ Related Plays
The alpha set:
• 48/49 G-zone
• 30/31 G
• 10/11 G
• 20/21 G

It's a small step to make from the trap to the trap option. On paper, and in practice, the trap option is a good play to feed the defense that has had it's fill of the standard trap. The playside defenders will ideally charge hard inside upon seeing the slot back dart in to get the ball and—they think—run the trap one more time (Figure 3-17). The quarterback's read will be the playside outside backer.

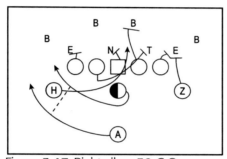

Figure 3-17. Right silver 30 G.O.

Up until the actual trap fake, backfield movements and paths are exactly the same as in the 30 G. The quarterback, instead of giving the ball to the incoming H-back, will pull the ball and attack the outside edge of the line of scrimmage. The A-back, who originally was faking a toss sweep, continues on his path and becomes the pitch back. The read options, of course, remain the same as in any option. If the outside backer crashes down hard, the quarterback pitches to the A-back. If not, the quarterback will tuck the ball away and sprint through the crease. Remember, an option that is drawn out wide is an option that fails.

The line play remains the same as in the 30 G, even including the same trap block on the defensive tackle. The linebackers will get absolutely no at-the-snap read on this play. For all intents and purposes, they will see a normal trap and will hopefully stream toward the center of the line. The left tackle will block the defensive end, hopefully hooking him and forcing him inside. Variations on this play are shown in Figures 3-18 and 3-19.

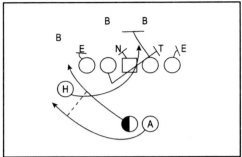

Figure 3-18. Right black slot rip gun 30 G.O.

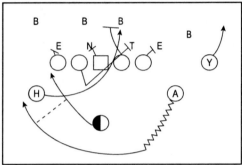

Figure 3-19. Right tiger gun 30 G.O. A-In

24/25 and 34/35 GT

☐ Related Plays
   The omega set:
      • 44/45 G
      • 14/15 G
      • 28/29 Zone
      • 38/39 Zone

The counter, along with the trap, is the mainstay of any running offense. The spread bone uses the slot back counter and the A-back power as the basis of its omega set. Like all of the 20/30 series, the counter is presented from the base formation, silver, and uses the H-back (Figure 3-20).

On the snap of the ball, the quarterback will reverse out, gaining as little depth as possible so the A-back will fake the offside power, his responsibility extending past the play fake to blocking the offside defensive end. His fake complete, the quarterback will offer the ball to the outside, to the approaching H-back. That slot back takes a slightly

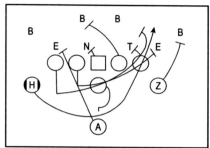

Figure 3-20. Right silver 34 GT

different path than on the alpha set traps. He takes a deep drop step at the snap, circling down toward the mesh—where the quarterback and running back meet—enabling him to attack the target hole at a sharp angle.

The counter relies upon a backside GT pull. The left guard, the quickest lineman, will pull and kick out the last man on the defensive line, usually the defensive end. The left tackle will pull and dive up into the hole, looking to seal off any inside-out pursuit by blocking the playside inside linebacker. Playside linemen, as a rule, block down—the center, in this case, on the offside tackle/nose, the right guard on the backside linebacker, and the right tackle on his defensive counterpart. The play ide defensive end is left unblocked, an easy kick-out block for the pulling offensive guard. The playside slot back, in this case the Z-back, advances to block the playside outside linebacker and to prevent him from reaching the inside run.

The omega set, unlike the alpha set, can easily be run out of the shotgun with a few minor adjustments. The only change comes with the manner of the slot back's receipt of the ball—instead of a handoff, use a quick inside shovel. Figures 3-21 and 3-22 show two examples of the counter out of the shotgun.

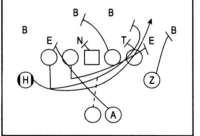

Figure 3-21. Right silver gun rip 34 GT

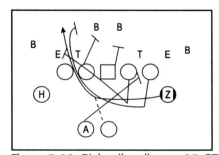

Figure 3-22. Right silver liz gun 25 GT

28/29 and 38/39 Zone

The slot back sweep, or 28/29 and 38/39 zone, is the third and last major component of the omega set (the other two components being, of course, the power and the counter). Figure 3-23 illustrates the slot back sweep as the natural response to a defense that is stacking up against the counter and the power.

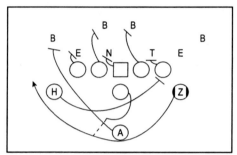

Figure 3-23. Right silver 29 zone

The backfield movement sticks to the paths outlined in the counter; the quarterback reverses out, faking the power to the A-back and the counter overtop to the H-back. The H-back, it needs to be understood, continues his counter path and is responsible for blocking any threats at the end of the line of scrimmage, which should be the unblocked defensive end. The A-back's responsibility is almost the exact opposite; he bends his path to the outside of the line of scrimmage while looking to reach and hook the first outside threat, most probably the outside linebacker.

The Z-back has, at the snap, taken a hard step toward the sidelines, pivoting on the second step to loop back deep into the backfield. For some athletes, it may prove easier to take a simple counter step rather than a pivot-step. The quarterback, having given his two fakes, will flip the ball in the option-style toward the Z-back, who will continue around the end, cutting the ball up the field at any available outside crease.

The linemen, on sweep blocking, will zone block to the playside, placing the offensive front five on the nearest defensive five. Remember, the offside defensive end is blocked by the H-back as he completes his counter fake. All blockers are attempting to reach and hook their respective defenders.

This play can be run out of a variety of formations and with a variety of motions. Figure 3-24 illustrates a true jet sweep look out of a one slot set. Additionally, only minor adjustments need to be made to run the play out of a shotgun formation. The H-back has to know to keep his counter path shallow, while the Z-back needs to make sure that he is deeper than the crossing H-back. The sweep pitch from the quarterback is an underneath shovel flip. A variation on this play is shown in Figure 3-25.

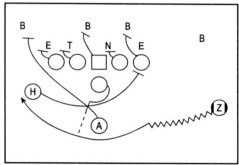

Figure 3-24. Right black slot z-thru 29 zone

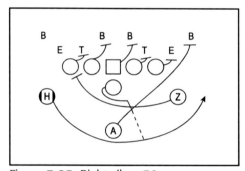

Figure 3-25. Right silver 38 zone

The 40 Series: The A-Back

44/45 G

☐ Related Plays
The omega set:
- 24/25 GT
- 34/35 GT
- 14/15 G
- 28/29 Zone
- 38/39 Zone

The A-back power is one of the spread bone's basic power plays, run in the exact same manner as the quarterback power reviewed in the section on the 10 series. On the snap, the quarterback will reverse out, dropping to a depth of two yards behind the line of scrimmage, and offer the ball to the approaching A-back (Figure 3-26). The A-back has attacked the mesh point without hesitation, his target the playside tackle. Once clear of the line of scrimmage, the A-back should read his kick and seal blocks, looking to slash through the second level between the playside linebacker and the playside outside linebacker.

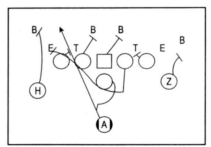

Figure 3-26. Right silver 45 G

That playside outside linebacker is the blocking responsibility of the playside slot, the H-back, who should endeavor to turn his man out and drive him to the sidelines. The offside slot, the Z-back, drops down to the line of scrimmage to replace the offside tackle and is responsible for blocking the last man on the defensive line, usually the end. Receivers should seek to run their defenders down the field, stalk-blocking them to the outside when the defenders react to the run.

Just as with the 14/15 G, the only pull involved is the offside guard, the right guard, who kicks out the end man on the line of scrimmage to the playside, usually the defensive end. All other linemen will zone block down with the exception of the backside tackle, who can be used to fall on the legs of the backside defensive tackle to penetration through the gap left by the pulling guard. The same adjustments made to the 14/15 G apply to the 44/45 G in shotgun and the other various non-silver one-back formations.

46/47 Zone

The quick pitch is a keen variation on the standard toss sweep, a play that relies mainly on reaching the outside crease between the outside linebacker and the interior line before the defense has a chance to react. This play can be run out of the standard A-back alignment, though a slight advantage can be gained by offsetting the A-back with a rip/liz call to the playside. At the snap, the quarterback sets his feet and quickly flips the ball nearly horizontally down the line toward the A-back (Figure 3-27). The A-back, meanwhile, has attacked the line of scrimmage just wide of the line of scrimmage, hitting the edge at full speed.

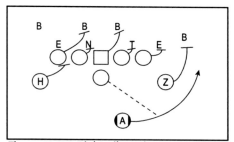

Figure 3-27. Right silver rip 46 zone

The line play has been left purposefully simple to let it adapt to any given defensive situation. As a rule, every member of the offense, save for the receivers, will zone block to the right. In this case, the Z-back will reach and kick the outside backer toward the sidelines, while his offside counterpart, the H-back, will replace the LT on the line of scrimmage, blocking the defensive end. The playside tackle, the right tackle, will attempt to hook the playside defensive end, with the right guard on the defensive tackle. The center will attempt to reach the playside linebacker. The backside linemen will zone block.

48/49

48/49 zone is a true power sweep, the big brother of the quick pitch. Like all of the spread bone's zone plays, the blocking scheme is extremely simple at the conceptual level. The power sweep relies on the speed of your A-back and the blocking ability of your linemen rather than any kind of misdirection or deception. In a way, the zone plays in the 40 series are an aberration of the spread bone philosophy; two talent-oriented plays amidst a game plan based on the flex bone philosophy of misdirection. The 48/49 zone is one of the simplest plays in the spread bone arsenal.

On taking the snap, the quarterback will reverse out and give a dead pitch to the sweeping A-back, whose target is the sideline (Figure 3-28). This play is one of the few in the spread bone that is designed to hit wide. The key blocks come from the playside slot, in this case the H-back, and the playside tackle. Their zone blocks are the most important, and, if carried off successfully, will free up the outside to the A-back. The H-back will zone to the outside to either block or cut the outside backer, while the left tackle should zone and hook the playside defensive end. The remaining linemen will follow their standard zone play rules, stepping hard to the playside and picking up or hooking any defensive player in that zone.

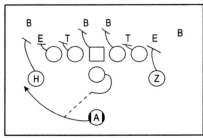

Figure 3-28. Right silver 49 zone

48/49 G-Zone

☐ Related Plays
The alpha set:
- 10/11 G
- 30/31 G
- 30/31 G.O.
- 20/21 G
- 20/21 G.O.

The last play of the alpha set in the spread bone playbook is the trap sweep. Like its conceptual brethren, the trap option, 48/49 G-zone is designed to strike suddenly to the outside while the defense is reacting to a threat inside. Additionally, the blocking and back movement remain similar to the rest of the alpha set.

The quarterback will take the snap and reverse out, faking the immediate toss sweep to the A-back and moving to fake the trap-give to the incoming H-back (Figure 3-29). Just like the trap option, the quarterback will pull the ball instead of giving the handoff and will flip the ball out to the A-back. The A-back has continued on his sweep path and receives the pitch when he is already wider than the outside defender on the line of scrimmage. It's important that the quarterback ride the trap as long as possible before finally flipping the ball out to the A-back to really sell the inside run. The trap sweep is also the reason that the A-back must, must, must give the same effort to his sweep fake in the rest of the alpha set—the sight of the sweeping A-back will not clue a defender in to the nature of the play.

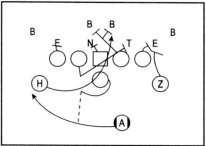
Figure 3-29. Right silver rip 49 G-zone

The line play remains the same as on the 30 G. The left guard will trap block on the defensive tackle while the center, the right guard, and the right tackle will block down. The Z-back will fill in and block the last man on the offside, the defensive end. The only new type of block falls to the quarterback, who will release outside to block or cut the outside linebacker.

Grant Halverson/Getty Images

The line play remains the same as on the 30 G.

The Specials Series

100/200 QB Draw and 80/90 Draw

☐Related Series
100/200 Half-roll drop

One of the most obvious running plays out of the spread is the common quarterback draw, which stretches the defense horizontally and vertically, fakes the half-roll drop, and lets the defense take itself out of position by reacting to the pass. The 80/90 series, meanwhile, is based off of the quicker three-step drop pass. It needs to be pointed out that the A-back/QB draw is not a good play to run against an inside stunt through the A-gaps. Your team needs to have a handy check if the quarterback reads a blitz at the center of the line, ideally two shallow crossing routes across the middle of the field to take advantage of the vacated space.

The quarterback draw also benefits from a presnap read and audible at the line of scrimmage, especially when given a four-man front as in Figure 3-30. When given a slanted nose/tackle look (i.e., the inside defenders in a 1 and a 3 technique), the quarterback needs to call the play away from the slanted nose. Upon seeing the defensive front in the Figure 3-30, for example, the quarterback should call a 200-series pass.

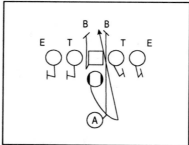

Figure 3-30. Right gold 200 QB draw

The example given illustrates a standard split defense without a hard A-gap rush. At the snap of the ball, all linemen save the center will use their standard BOB blocking rules, meaning that if the center is attacked, one man has come uncovered, most likely a tackle, and the tackle must now assume the center's draw responsibilities. The center will show pass for one count before charging at the playside backer, either hooking him or taking him to the sidelines, depending on his angle. The quarterback, at the snap, has taken his quick three-step (or half-roll) drop, eyes up the field, handing off to the waiting A-back at his third step (or, conversely, following the A-back's lead block up through the hole).

The receivers (X, Y, Z, and H-back) should run their routes at full speed, seeking to run their respective defenders down the field. The split ends, the X and Y, will run go routes down the field, while the slot backs should run the three-step shoot route in an attempt to pull the outside backers even further toward the sidelines.

700/800 G

☐Related Plays
  700/800 series: Screen game

The 700/800 G is used to exploit a defense that has seen your successful bubble/ jailbreak screen pass numerous times. It's a quick play that relies upon the defense reacting to the quarterback's distinctive bubble/jailbreak screen passing motion to free up the interior to your quickest back.

Back motion is simple. The quarterback rises up and pump-fakes the bubble screen to the playside, continues to reverse out, and gives the ball to the charging A-back (Figure 3-31). The line play differs from the rest of the spread bone trap plays; the 700/800 G features more of a fold block than a true G trap.

The center will block down on the playside tackle, while the left guard will fold over and block the offside inside linebacker. The remaining blockers on the playside, the left tackle and the H-back, will each zone step right, away from the call. The left tackle scramble blocks the playside defensive tackle, while the H-back will collapse and fill on the line of scrimmage, blocking the defensive end. The right tackle and right guard will base block.

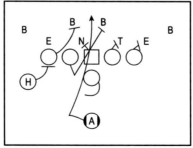

Figure 3-31. Right black slot 800 G

300/400 Zone

☐Related Plays
  300/400 series: Sprint passes

The sprint-out sweep is a new kind of play, of a type that usually manifests itself as a draw rather than a toss sweep. Like the 700/800 G, the 300/400 zone takes advantage of a distinctive quarterback movement to draw the defense away from the true object of the play. In its mechanics and theory, the 400 zone resembles the old Statue of Liberty play.

Like any zone play, 300/400 zone relies upon a zone-step block from its offensive linemen and the two slot backs. The finesse comes, not in the simplified blocking scheme, but in the quarterback and A-back interaction on the sprint-out fake. The quarterback will take the snap and truly sprint toward the outside of the pocket at full speed, eyes downfield (Figure 3-32). The A-back, meanwhile, takes two shuffle steps to the right, as if looking to protect the outside edge of the pocket, and then moves to take the ball from the sprinting quarterback. The handoff occurs behind the quarterback in an attempt to disguise the possession change as much as possible. Ball firmly in hand, the A-back will streak around the end, following his zone blocks. The 300/400 zone tries to capture the best of both worlds by giving a play-fake off of the quarterback's sprint-out motion while still giving the A-back every possibility of getting to the corner with a full zone block from the offensive line.

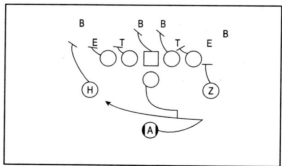

Figure 3-32. Right silver 400 zone

The Tiger Series

The truest incarnation of the spread offense is the "empty" set, a formation incorporating an empty backfield and five wideouts. The trouble most spread teams have with an empty set is getting any kind of running game out of it without a complex change of terminology or personnel. The spread bone offense, however, utilizes the tiger series as a balanced set, equally divided between running and passing plays—without needless complexity or personnel change. In fact, spread bone players should find no difficulty in running the normal running playbook, with slight adjustment, out of the tiger series. The key comes in ensuring that all players understand that any given play out of the tiger series is run in the same manner as if run out of any other formation; the same players will hit the same paths, same motions, same blocks, and same holes.

The tiger series could just as easily have been called white, or empty, or nickel-wide, but it gains its distinctive name from its aggressive personality. The tiger series is coming after you, whether in the air or on the ground—and it cannot be stopped. Essentially, going into tiger only robs the spread bone of one potential runner, the Z-back, who goes out wide as a split receiver. Thus, the offense still retains three possible ball handlers and is still fully capable of running the entire ground attack playbook.

In any tiger series running play, the A-back is called into an "in" motion, a short motion into his typical position in the backfield. From this position, any 10/30/40 series play can be run with no adjustment by the backfield or the linemen. Of course, one can argue that this isn't truly running out of an empty set, since you're motioning a back into the backfield. However, the enterprising offensive coordinator can motion the A-back all the way across the formation to flood a passing zone or, indeed, motion the A-back in and then back out into a route to confuse the defense. The important thing is maintaining the simplicity of the offense without using an abundance of different personnel.

Figure 3-33 illustrates how the motioning A-back is right in position to continue his option path with the quarterback. Figure 3-34 demonstrates a running play involving the slot back, the H-back. Figure 3-35 illustrates the ability to run the trap and trap option. The rules and adjustments for going into shotgun still apply when running a play out of the tiger series. Figure 3-36 exemplifies this point.

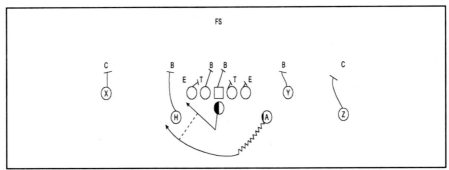

Figure 3-33. Right tiger 17 O

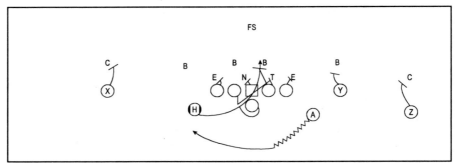

Figure 3-34. Right tiger 30 G

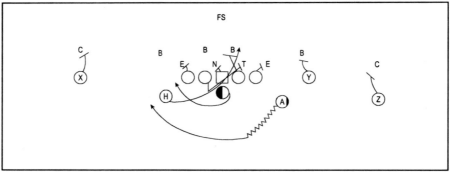

Figure 3-35. Right tiger 30 G.O.

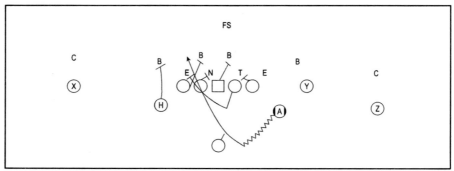

Figure 3-36. Right tiger gun 45 G

4

The Passing Game

"It's starting to come together, Pepper."

—Lou Brown (James Gammon) in *Major League*

The watchword when it comes to the spread bone passing attack is "patience," though this is a virtue easier claimed than practiced. Patience in this context is the act of recognizing and taking what you are given by a defense. In practice, patience in the spread passing game means taking the short, controlled, quick strikes over the deep post if that is where the defense's weakness lies. In truth, this kind of patience is at the heart of the West Coast–style passing attack. Traditionally, the spread has been known more for its deep strike capability than the controlled passing game. However, having the patience to take the short gain over and over again, while simultaneously using the run to set up the play-action pass, is what the spread bone is all about. The mastery of this kind of patience is rewarded in two kinds of currency, the kinds that appeals to a football coach the most: touchdowns and victories.

So how do you take what you are given? In the spread bone, this is done through five different passing series: the three-step drop, the five-step (or half-roll) drop, the sprint-out pass, the play-action pass, and the screen. Each passing series is designed to create different scoring opportunities. The three-step series is designed for the quick hits reminiscent of the west coast offense. The five-step, half-roll series is used to stretch the field and create passing windows—the rapier to bleed the defense white. The sprint-out series is used to place the quarterback on the edge as a true run-pass threat, while the play-action series is used to complement the running game and produce downfield opportunities by tricking the defense into committing to the run. Finally, the screen game is used for high-percentage throws, quick and to the edge, to give the receiver the possibility of large gains.

The examples provided in this chapter use various formations to illustrate the various possibilities. As with Chapter 3, not all formations or defense responses are shown. Remember, this book is meant to be a starting point and a basic reference, not the be-all and end-all of the spread passing game. Furthermore, the line play is not discussed for the three-step, five-step, and sprint-out series as it can be found in the Chapter 2 under the section on offensive line play.

The Three-Step Series: 80s and 90s

For true simplicity, look no further than the spread bone's three-step series. These simple route combinations can be excellent short-yardage, quick-strike passes ideal for use against man-coverage or against a zone with a deep cushion. Figure 4-1 illustrates a hitch pattern. The quarterback will look to the Z receiver first, who has attacked the outside shoulder of the outside linebacker and curled back to the inside. This outside release should create enough space between the inside linebacker and the outside linebacker to provide a lane for the quarterback. The H-back will run the route exactly the same on the backside. In fact, all receivers will run the called route. In Figure 4-2, simplicity is the key, as it for the entire three-step series. This is the perfect attack for a press cover 2 or cover 3. Like the previous example, the H and Z-backs are the primary targets, forcing the free safety to choose which to cover. The quarterback should use his eyes to pull the free safety to one side and then hit the opposite receiver at 18 to 20 yards in the seam.

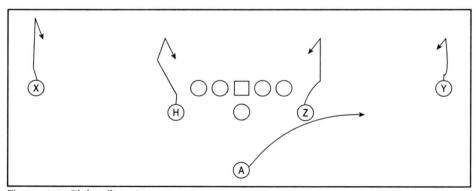

Figure 4-1. Right silver 80

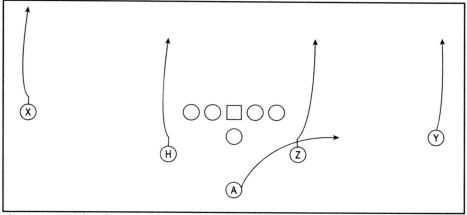

Figure 4-2. Right silver 99

The Five-Step Series: 100s and 200s

"Simplicity" will be a reoccurring theme in every aspect of the spread bone passing game. In these examples, the simplicity does not lie in the routes, but rather in the decision-making process of the quarterback. Against any pass coverage windows will always exist. Against cover 3, the offense wants to attack the outside linebacker. In the following plays, that is done by threatening the flats, the outside linebackers' pass-responsibility in cover 3, and then coming over the top with the dig or curl route and "replacing" the vacant outside linebacker's place on the field. The reads against cover 3 are simple: if the outside linebacker flows then the quarterback throws the dig, if the outside linebacker sits and stays then the quarterback throws the shoot route. This system of attacking cover 3 is demonstrated in Figure 4-3.

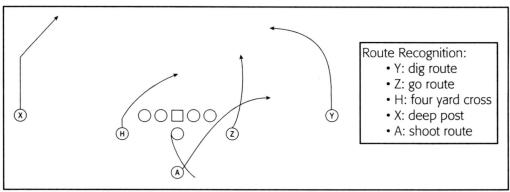

Route Recognition:
 • Y: dig route
 • Z: go route
 • H: four yard cross
 • X: deep post
 • A: shoot route

Figure 4-3. Right silver 239

All passes in the 100/200 series are from a five-step, or half-roll, drop, meaning that the quarterback will, by the end of his drop, have completed a slight roll out to the playside (ideally setting up to pass behind his guards). An example of the entire series would be the aptly named choice route, 1/209 in the spread bone terminology. The route combination offers route variations against specific coverages and alignments. The ability to change and adapt routes allows the offense to exploit a defensive scheme at its weakest point. Throughout this book, simplicity has been the key. While a read-and-react passing attack can appear daunting at the surface level, it is in fact merely a series of obvious checks that can simplify the offensive process once the scheme is understood by all.

Against a 30 zone or cover 3 coverage, the X and Y will maintain their called routes, offering the hitch, or zero route, underneath the deep corner and outside linebacker. The check occurs against press cover 2 or man press coverage. If the corner is within five yards of the receiver, press coverage should be recognized, and the quarterback and receiver should check the hitch to a fade or seven route. The check can be either verbal or through hand signals. However the check occurs, it must be repeated and recognized by both the quarterback and receiver to avoid any miscommunication.

The H-back and Z-back, like the X and Y, will not check their route against cover 3 zone coverage; both will run along the outside of the hash. The quarterback should recognize the zone coverage, and most importantly the single safety, and use his eyes to draw the free safety to one side and throw back across to the opposite receiver, away from the covering safety. The ball should be delivered at 18 to 20 yards. This quick strike throw will clear the dropping linebackers and prevent the safety from playing both routes.

Against cover 2 zone coverage, the H-back and Z-back must read the safety. If the safety flows to the fade route, then the Z-back or H-back will continue on path. However, if the safety stays over the top of the H-back or Z-back, then the receivers will read the safety as either "hard" or "soft," depending on his proximity to the receiver and his backpedal. A hard safety has given little ground to the H-back or Z-back in his backpedal, which has allowed the receiver to close on the defender. In this situation, the receiver will continue on his path and run past the flatfooted defender. The soft safety, on the other hand, has played very loose and has continued to drop. He is essentially trying to keep the H-back or Z-back in front of him. Against this look, the receiver will push his route to about 12 to 15 yards and then settle it down as a curl route. It is important for the receiver to find the window to the quarterback. As a general rule, if the receiver cannot see the quarterback as he curls, then he is not open. The receiver must work into the quarterback's line of sight.

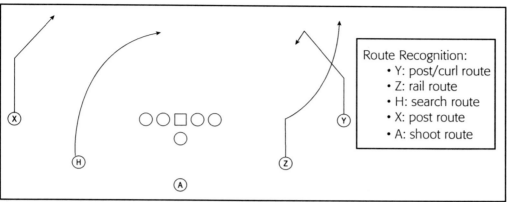

Figure 4-4. Right black 257

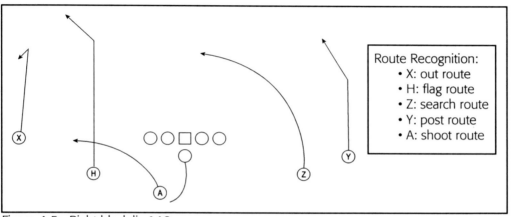

Figure 4-5: Right black liz 146

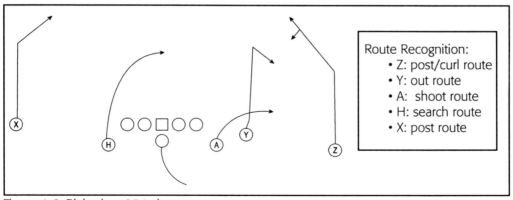

Figure 4-6. Right tiger 254 shoot

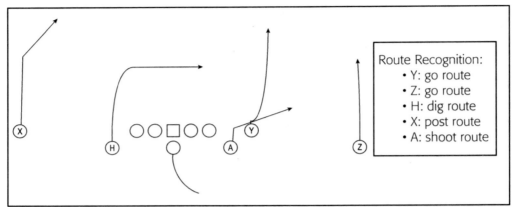

Figure 4-7. Right tiger 299 shoot

The Sprint-Out Series: 300s and 400s

The sprint-out package is a great addition to the passing game for any team. The ability to get your quarterback on the edge as a run-pass threat creates opportunity, especially if your quarterback is a legitimate athlete and your passing game has been hurting the defense. The sprint-out package, by its nature, is really an option play, in that the quarterback has the option to throw the ball or to continue around the end. The defense has to be able to defend both options, and for many defenses, especially defenses that have faced the spread bone for an entire game, the sprint out will start taking a heavy toll.

Simplicity is also the key to the sprint-out game. Much like the five-step series, the sprint-out series is centered on attacking specific areas of zone coverage, in this case the flats and the hook-to-curl zone. Figures 4-8 through 4-12 illustrate how to attack cover 3 using the sprint-out series within the spread bone offense.

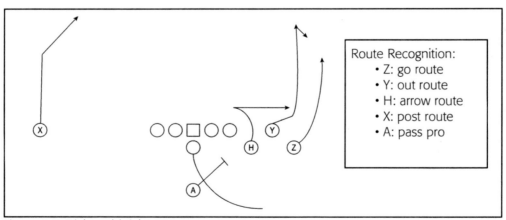

Figure 4-8. Right gold tight 494 arrow

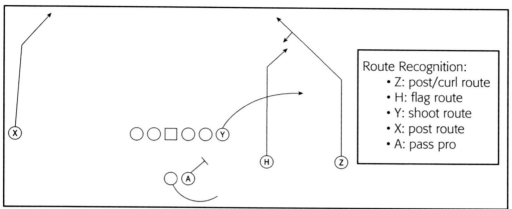

Figure 4-9. Right red gun rip 456 shoot

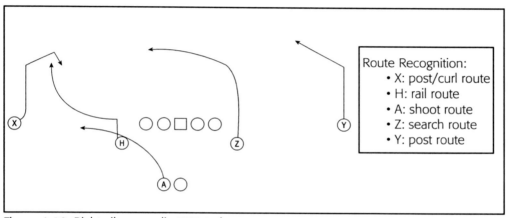

Figure 4-10. Right silver gun liz 357 A-shoot

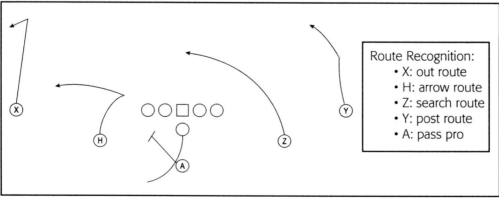

Figure 4-11. Right black 348

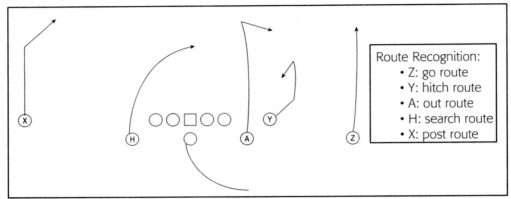

Figure 4-12. Right tiger 490 out

The Play-Action Series: 500s and 600s

The play-action pass is a great tool for any offense. Within the spread bone, three route combinations are used: normal (assumed without a call), switch, and search. These variations are used to attack the defense with multiple route combinations off of similar play-actions. The rules for each combination are as follows.

Normal

This basic sequence is the most commonly used route combination. The outside receiver to the roll side runs a 15 yard out. If the number two receiver is to the roll side he runs a flag, and if he is away from the roll side he runs a drag (Figure 4-13). If the number three receiver is to the roll call he runs a shoot route, and if he is away from the roll call he runs a post route.

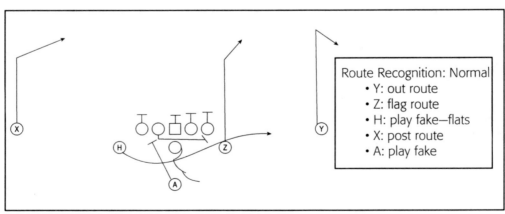

Figure 4-13. Right silver 634

Switch

This route combination is illustrated in Figure 4-14, in which the number one and number two receivers' route assignments switch. The number one receiver now runs a go route. The number two runs an out route. The number three receiver still runs a shoot route. This call would only be made if multiple receivers are to the roll side.

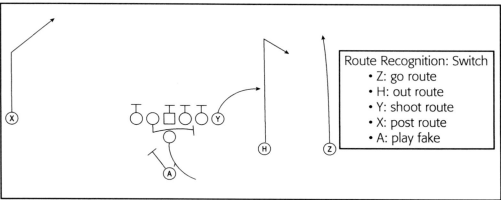

Figure 4-14. Right red 643 switch

Search

The number one receiver runs a search route. The number two receiver runs a rail route, and the number three receiver runs a go route. This combination would also be used only when multiple receivers are to the roll side (Figure 4-15).

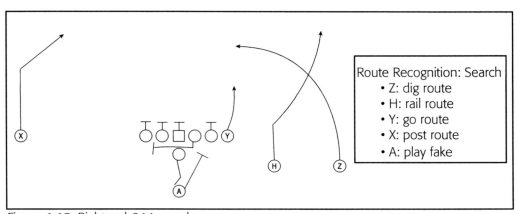

Figure 4-15. Right red 644 search

While varying route combinations are critical to play-action, true success is found in the offensive line play. The key to making a good play-fake on the line is to not fall immediately into pass protection. Instead, lineman will "man up" at the line of scrimmage, taking the nearest threat as their responsibility (nearest lineman or linebacker, similar to BOB blocking rules). At the snap, they will fire out and engage the defensive man as if run blocking. On the second beat, however, they must learn not to drive but to yield and, above all, keep their hands on their man. Also, the playside guard (the guard the play fake is being run to) always pulls at the snap and heads to cut the man at the endangered opposite edge. The A-back, meanwhile, fills the guard's vacated spot (most likely necessitating a cut block). To summarize, linemen attack and yield while the guard and A-back pull and replace.

The Screen Series: 700s and 800s

The screen game is a critical part of any passing offense. In the spread bone it is used as a high-percentage pass with the hope of a large return. In the basic package, two different schemes are employed: the backdoor and the read.

Backdoor Series

The backdoor series is when an offense is in a three-receiver set, whether motioning a receiver across the field or simply lining up in a straight trips formation. The number-2 receiver, or the motion man, will be the recipient of the screen pass. In Figure 4-16, the H-back is the receiver as stated in the play call. The other frontside receivers will run a post and the number-3 receiver will run a rail route. At the snap of the ball, the H-back will come underneath the line and settle on the other side of the weak tackle. The quarterback will sprint out to the call side, settle just outside the tackle, turn, locate, and throw. The A-back will maintain his normal sprint-out responsibilities, as does the frontside guard and tackle. The center and backside guard and tackle will gate protect for a two-count, and then release to the second level, picking up first threat.

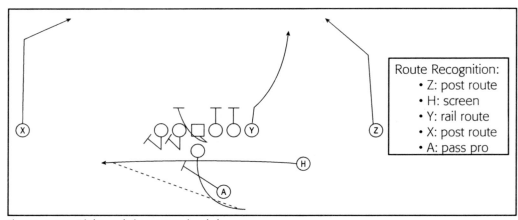

Figure 4-16. Right red rip 700 H backdoor

Read Series

The read series can be run to a two- or three-receiver formation. The quarterback is going to read the playside cornerback and call the play at the line. If the corner is playing loose, six to eight yards, then the QB wants to call the bubble. If the corner is playing tight, then the QB wants to call the jailbreak. This read system works because the assignments are very simple. For the bubble screen, the number one receiver blocks man on and the number two is the receiver. After the catch the number two will read the block and get upfield as quickly as possible. The jailbreak screen incorporates the playside tackle into the blocking assignment. The number one receiver will receive the pass and the number two receiver will block back on number one's man (cornerback). The tackle will release to the number two defender (safety or outside linebacker). If both receivers are being pressed, then the quarterback must audible to another play.

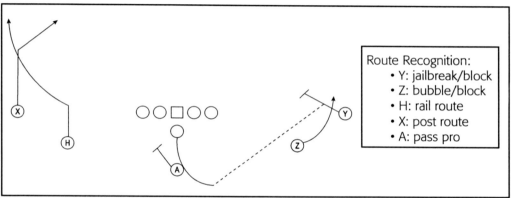

Figure 4-17. Right black 800 read (bubble)

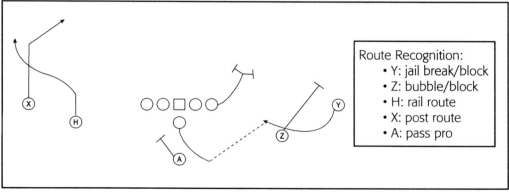

Figure 4-18. Right black 800 read (jailbreak)

5

The Rocket/Laser and Ram/Lion Series

"Fortune favors the bold."
—Virgil

The Shotgun Attack Out of the Spread Bone

Throughout this book, taking the snap directly from center has been advocated as the most desirable option for a team, especially given the wing-t oriented approach to back movement. However, it must be recognized that most teams are attracted to the spread offense precisely because it allows them to operate from the shotgun and, by extension, allows a weaker offensive line a chance to be successful pass blockers by placing the quarterback some yards from the defense. While most plays from the spread bone can be run from either under center or from the shotgun with a little manipulation (a shovel pass substituting for a handoff, in most instances), the need for a purely shotgun-only oriented running game is paramount, both to give the defense another look and to bolster the play of a weaker offensive line. The spread bone's rocket/laser and ram/lion series are designed to provide just such an attack from the shotgun, while keeping entirely within the rules of the offense as laid out earlier in this book.

The advantages of a spread-type shotgun run offense are obvious. First, it lends itself to the spread passing game extremely well, forcing defenses to prepare equally for an attack by ground or air. Second, it provides an offense specifically designed to counter what could be considered as a weak offensive line. The shotgun snap delivers the football to the mesh point of the play instantly, preventing catastrophic blocking failure by the offensive line from being necessarily destructive. In other words, the back is given the ball with enough time and space to make his own cut decisions should his line-blocking fail. Also, a busted guard or tackle pull will not force the back off his attack path as it will with typical wing-t running plays. For example, how many times have you seen a pulling guard blown up by a stunting linebacker and forced backward into the slot back during a slot back trap? The shotgun allows the line a moment's weakness, the room to recover, and the time to make their blocks. Likewise, it allows the backs the time to adjust to a failure in the protection up front.

The base formation for the rocket/laser and ram/lion series is the double slot look the spread bone calls silver. Both series require a quarterback in the shotgun, an off-set A-back, and a presnap motion. To simplify play calling, all of these conditions are included in one word (either "rocket" or "laser," or "ram" or "lion") instead of being expressly stated. For example, right silver gun liz becomes simply right silver rocket. It is understood that the quarterback is in the gun and that the A-back is off set to the quarterback's right (in other words, to the play call designated by the rocket, for "right," call). The term rocket/laser refers to a presnap jet sweep–type motion for either the H-back or Z-back (Figure 5-1). The term ram/lion refers to a presnap deep option–type motion from the same two backs (Figure 5-2). Both motions must cross the center; thus, in right silver laser, the quarterback is in the gun, the A-back is offset to his left, and the Z-back is going in a hard jet sweep–type motion to his left (as designated by the "laser" call).

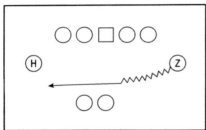

Figure 5-1. Rocket/laser motion

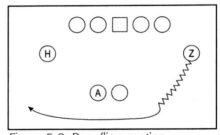

Figure 5-2. Ram/lion motion

Regardless of the actual play, all back paths out of rocket or laser (with one exception) are the same. The slot back away from the motion call (for instance, the left slot back if the call is rocket) will go into a hard motion across the formation and either get the ball. on a jet-sweep or fake receiving the ball while dashing around the end of the line.

The A-back will always either receive or fake a counter handoff, aiming for the opposite tackle/end gap. This may require a hard counter step away from the eventual target gap at the snap, depending on individual timing. The quarterback's path is the only one that may vary. After faking a jet sweep and a counter, he may be called on to sprint up the middle on a short trap, or around the end, following the sweeping slot back's block, on a quarterback sweep. The non-ballcarrying slot back will either drop down to the line to cover a pulling guard/tackle (if the play is away) or attempt to zone-hook the end or outside linebacker.

The rocket/laser and ram/lion series also have a simplified play designation system to avoid confusing a base spread bone play from a rocket/laser play that technically should bear the same name. Since the back paths in the rocket/laser series are always the same regardless of the actual play, the only calls that need to be made are those that reference line blocking and assignments. An example of a play call from the rocket/laser series is right silver rocket zone, which refers to a double-slot formation, a shotgun/back-offset/slot back motion, and a full zone block from the linemen. Since the paths of the backs never change, designating a ballcarrier and a target hole is not only redundant but potentially confusing. The ram/lion series has a bit more variation in the back paths from play to play, but the play calling will remain as simplified as possible.

The Rocket/Laser Series

Rocket/Laser Zone

The most obvious play that can be run out of a jet-sweep motion is the simple jet sweep (Figure 5-3). The quarterback must call for the snap with perfect timing. Ideally, the ball arrives in the quarterback's hands at the same moment the sweeping slot back is crossing the mesh point. Taking the jet-sweep handoff from the quarterback, the slot back will attempt to turn upfield after he hits the perimeter of the defense, following his blocking. Meanwhile, the quarterback and A-back should carry out their assigned rocket/laser back paths, faking the counter-trap.

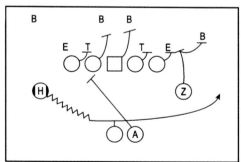

Figure 5-3. Right silver rocket zone

Should the playside defensive end align himself head up or outside of the blocking slot back, that back will attempt to zone-step and hook that end. Should the defensive end be lined up inside of the slot back in a 5 technique, the slot back will engage him with the objective of sliding off to block the playside outside linebacker. If the playside offensive tackle is capable, the slot back may even forego the chip block entirely on a 5 technique and try and reach the outside linebacker immediately upon the snap. All offensive linemen should, as the play call indicates, take a hard zone step to the playside and try to "reach" an entire gap or man over. By design, the linebackers should, after seeing multiple plays out of the rocket/laser series, be frozen by the countering back paths, giving linemen time to make blocks and the sweeping slot back time to reach the edge and turn upfield.

Rocket/Laser GT

The rocket/laser series gets its power and effectiveness from the elaborate crossing and counter-movement of the backs. In essence, this shotgun run offense is designed to confuse or freeze the linebackers in their tracks in addition to providing a chance for a small offensive line to succeed. If the most basic play in the series is the jet sweep, the natural offshoot is the A-back counter-trap, or, to use spread bone terminology, the rocket/laser GT (Figure 5-4).

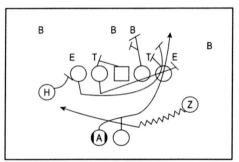

Figure 5-4. Right silver laser GT

Like all rocket/laser plays, the back motion incorporates a jet sweep motion from the opposite slot back. In the case of the GT, the quarterback will fake the jet sweep handoff to the motioning slot back, then offer the ball to the off-set A-back. It is imperative that the sweeping slot back continues on his designated path, selling the jet sweep to the defense, particularly to the linebackers. Again, the A-back may need to take an initial counter-step depending on individual timing before he turns playside to take the handoff. Once he has the ball, the slot back will aim for the tackle/end gap.

The blocking up front remains the same as on any of the spread bone's GT plays. Basically, the playside linemen, including the center, will block down hard, influencing the defensive end up the field. The backside guard and tackle will pull. The guard, first to arrive at the scene of attack, will kick out the influenced defensive end while the tackle will lead up inside the hole and attempt to seal off any backside defenders (most likely a middle linebacker). If the defensive is closing down hard with the unoccupied outside linebacker (the playside linebacker), the pulling tackle can be ordered to forego the seal block and instead kick out or log the first off-colored jersey that shows in the hole. The non-sweeping slot back will come down hard to the line of scrimmage to wash down or impede the progress of the backside defensive end. Cutting may be appropriate in this scenario.

An alternative to the GT is the simple rocket/laser GT read (Figure 5-5), which makes two slight changes to the standard GT to allow for a slightly different look. First, the slot back that is not in motion will no longer collapse and try to fill on the offensive line. Instead, he will release and try to block the outside linebacker, who should already be widening due to the jet-sweep motion of the other slot back. Meanwhile, the quarterback will ride the handoff with the countering A-back, eyes on the defensive end away from the counter's point of attack. Should that defensive end see the guard and tackle pull and, unblocked, rush upfield toward the mesh point, the quarterback should pull the ball and sweep around the now unprotected flank, aided by the end's lack of contain and the slot back's block. If the end should keep his composure and close with the offensive tackle, remaining on station at the far edge of the line, the quarterback should let the A-back take the ball on the counter-trap.

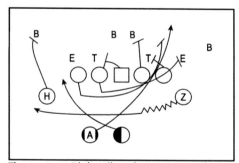
Figure 5-5. Right silver laser GT read

Rocket/Laser G

The effect of the crossing backs in the rocket/laser series is to widen the potential attack zone in the middle of the field. Often, the linebackers will spread at the snap to the various ends of the defensive line, leaving a gaping hole up the middle that can be exploited by the third potential ballcarrier, the quarterback.

After faking the jet sweep and the A-back counter, the quarterback will shoot up the middle of the field, aiming for the gap between the guard and the trapped tackle. It's wise to offer this play as a quarterback check, and have him call the trap to the side with the widest defensive tackle, most likely in a 3 technique (Figure 5-6). The various back motions and counters will have drawn the linebackers wide, allowing the quarterback to tuck the ball away and dart up the seam. A variation of this play can be to attack a wider gap—in effect, to trap the end rather than the tackle. In this variation, the quarterback would be hitting a hole on the same side as the sweeping slot back and opposite of the countering A-back.

Once again, line blocking remains the same as other traps in the spread bone. The playside end will turn out his man, while the playside guard and the center block down hard, the guard most likely reaching for a linebacker on the second level. The backside guard will pull and trap block the playside defensive tackle, kicking him out and away from the center of the line.

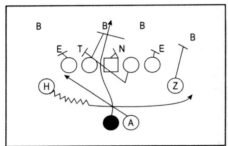

Figure 5-6. Right silver rocket G

After faking the jet sweep and the A-back counter, the quarterback will shoot up the middle of the field, aiming for the gap between the guard and the trapped tackle.

The Ram/Lion Series

Ram/Lion Zone

The ram/lion series places the motioning slot back in a different position to receive the ball than rocket and laser, and thus can be used to achieve what rocket and laser cannot. One such play is the ram/lion zone, a full-on power sweep look for a team looking to gain the corner quickly with the maximum amount of lead blocking at the edge (Figure 5-7).

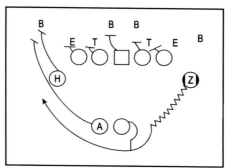

Figure 5-7. Right silver lion zone

As with any play out of ram or lion, presnap deep motion takes place with the designated slot back. This motion should take the back on a path behind the shotgun quarterback. It is truly a deep motion, but the distance the slot back will have to run to get back to the line of scrimmage is offset by the speed he will gain through the use of this motion. The quarterback should snap the ball when the motioning slot back is two steps away from him. Upon receiving the snap, the quarterback will execute a "reverse out," turning away from the play call and handing the ball off to the motioning slot back behind the mesh point—in essence hiding the exchange from the defense. The ballcarrier will then carry the ball around the end, trying to hit the corner and turn up, following his blockers. These blockers include the A-back, who will sweep out at the snap to become a lead blocker on the edge.

At the snap, the playside slot back should make his block according to the alignment of the defensive end. An end that is head up on or outside of the blocking slot back should be hooked, while an end lined up inside of the slot back should be engaged with the objective of chipping off to block the playside outside linebacker. Again, if the playside offensive tackle is more than capable of handling that defensive end, the slot back may try and reach the outside linebacker immediately upon the snap. All offensive linemen should take a hard zone step to the playside. The countering back paths of rocket/laser and ram/lion should freeze the linebackers, giving the linemen time to get a full hook on their respective blocks.

Ram/Lion GT

The counter out of ram or lion bears a strong resemblance to its rocket/laser equivalent. In fact, the difference lies only in the motion of the slot back and the mechanics of the handoff between the quarterback and the A-back (Figure 5-8). The quarterback will, upon receiving the shotgun snap, reverse out, turning his back to the defensive line for a split-second. It is not necessary to fake a handoff to the slot back in the deep ram/lion motion. The quarterback should continue his turn as if he had handed the ball off, and the slot back should continue on his power sweep path. Once the quarterback has completed his full turn he will offer the ball to the A-back, who has taken a single counter step at the snap and has turned back to receive the ball. As with the rocket/laser GT, the A-back will aim for the gap between the defensive end and the defensive tackle. In essence, the quarterback's pivot motion is very similar to that of a wing-t quarterback in that offense's slot back trap, turning almost 360 degrees before handing off the football. Line blocking does not vary from the rocket/laser GT. The playside of the line will block down, while the backside guard and tackle will pull and kick or seal.

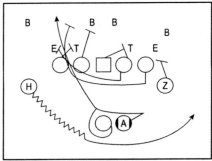

Figure 5-8. Right silver ram GT

Ram/Lion O

The ram/lion series provides an excellent opportunity for the option game out of the shotgun snap. Specifically, the O out of ram or lion becomes a load option, with at least two blockers coming out of the backfield to clear the way for the oncoming quarterback and slot back (Figure 5-9).

At the snap, the deep motion slot back becomes the pitch man, while the A-back will lead up on the outside edge and look to block the first off-colored jersey, most likely the outside linebacker. The playside slot back will collapse down to hook the end. In this version of the option, the quarterback will not be reading anything other than direct threats. If the quarterback feels threatened, he can pitch the ball out to the waiting deep motion slot back.

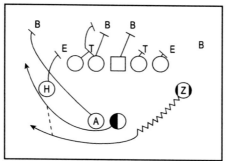

Figure 5-9. Right silver lion O

Line blocking remains faithful to the spread bone's normal option rules. The playside offensive linemen will block down, leaving the playside defensive end to be hooked by the slot back. Linemen on the backside will execute turn back protection, preventing anyone from shooting a gap and blowing the play up from the weakside.

A variation on the option theme is the ram/lion GTO, or the read option. This play is only recommended for teams with a quick-thinking, quick-reading quarterback. It proceeds in the much the same way as a ram/lion GT. On the snap, the quarterback will reverse out, facing the sweeping deep motion slot back, and, upon completion of his pivot, will read the play of the defensive end. Similar to the GT read of the rocket/laser series, the slot back will release outside to an outside linebacker while the backside guard and tackle will pull with the intention of kicking or sealing on a counter. If the defensive end comes hard up field, the quarterback should take the ball and continue around the end, pitching to the in-motion slot back if necessary. If the end is staying at home in his technique, the quarterback can give the A-back the ball on the counter. This play depends on the ability of the quarterback to quickly make a decision after completing his pivot. Even if he makes a wrong read, the opportunity of making a substantial gain is still present. The chances of a charging end making the tackle on a quick countering A-back are not high, and should the quarterback choose to run the option with a stay-at-home defensive end, that end becomes the pitch read.

The Passing Game out of Rocket/Laser or Ram/Lion

The spread bone passing game works equally well with the rocket/laser or ram/lion motion. The slot back in motion would, in essence, fill a receiver role (similar to a flanker motioning from a doubles formation into a trips formation). In rocket/laser, the slot back in motion would become the innermost receiver to the playside and would run the third tagged route. For example, in right silver rocket 299 go, the slot back receiver would run a go route (Figure 5-10).

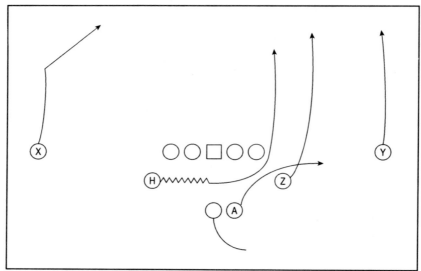

Figure 5-10. Right silver rocket 299 go

The pass rules for ram/lion are no different. The deep motion sets are not especially well-oriented to the passing game, but potentially can be effective.

6

Viewing the Gridiron as a Battlefield

"Where are the guns? Bring up the guns!"

—General James Longstreet at Gettysburg

In the fall of 331 B.C., an army of forty thousand men stood silently in battle rank, gazing across an arid plain at the massed horde of an enemy that outnumbered them at least six to one. They were Macedonians, the well-trained and well-seasoned veterans of Philip II and his prodigal son, Alexander, and they had marched all the way from mainland Greece to wrest the Persian Empire away from its native king, Darius III. They waited with the 16-foot spears called sarissas, a weapon unique to Macedon, in the tightly packed formation called the phalanx, a mode of fighting little understood by the Persians and honed to perfection by the battle-loving Macedonians. They were led by the most charismatic general the world had yet seen, a man to be known by history as Alexander the Great, a man who would ride at the head of his famed cavalry force, the Companions, and be the first to strike at the nearly invincible Persian infantry. Before this day in early October of 331 B.C., the Macedonians had never been defeated.

As discussed in Chapter 1, many coaches have a natural interest in military history that has led them into a career teaching history to a younger generation in addition to their duties on the practice field. The same type of mind is needed for both disciplines; the offensive coordinator and the field general are closer cousins then you might think.

The vocabulary of the sport reflects its basis in the violent, but controlled and directed, struggle between armored men on a field of battle. It follows, then, that the stratagems involved in a successful military campaign would also serve a football coach on the gridiron. The spread bone, specifically, takes its cues by treating the game as if it were a military battle, learning from the grand successes and dismal mistakes of generals and field marshals from ages past.

To begin, the spread bone follows a tenet held dear by all successful army commanders: overall numbers and talent count for nothing. What matters is outnumbering and outclassing the enemy at the point of attack. Coaches have always used this logic, even if they weren't conscious of it. The offense outlined in broad strokes in the pages of this book adopts this tenet as its basic philosophy. The talent, size, and speed of the opposing defense counts for nothing if you outnumber and outclass them at the critical juncture. What matter the Division I–caliber outside linebacker if you've schemed your game plan to run inside? What's more, what impact does a middle linebacker have if your back paths and line play are misleading enough to disguise the point of attack?
Hence, the second military tenet of the spread bone is to disguise the point of attack. Use misdirection to mislead the defense regarding where you are going to strike, and when you do strike, make sure the playing field favors your side and not your opponent. To this end the spread bone has adopted much of the misdirection of the wishbone and wing-t systems.

Remember, you are on offense, and your attitude must reflect that. A Department of Defense always has a hard time winning a conflict, while a War Department usually gets the job done. When attacking a foe that outnumbers him, a good commander does his level best to negate their numbers and their advantage. The spread is designed to spread the enemy thin and weaken his overall defense. Once his line has broken, once the offense penetrates the defensive line, victory is assured.

Consider Alexander's problem at the plain of Gaugamela. He is outnumbered. He is fighting on the Persian's home turf. The ground is flat and level and offers no opportunity to use the terrain to his advantage for an ambush. His troops are unsuited to the defensive; his is an attacking force, and to use such troops on the defensive cheapens their ability and weakens his army. Alexander must attack. No other options remain open to him.

His line of battle resembles the formation of a typical football team. In the middle he places his heavy infantry, the Macedonian phalanx, the equivalent of the offensive linemen of the modern game. On the wings are his cavalry divisions, though it is on his right wing that the dreaded Companions form up with Alexander at their head. Specially trained and lightly armed infantry men also form up on these wings, used to keep pace with the horses and attack the enemy simultaneously from an unexpected quarter. In essence, they are shock troops that are the Macedonian equivalents of running backs.

Alexander's plan is simple. While the phalanx occupies the center of the Persian line, trying to bull their way through and clear holes for penetration, Alexander leads his right wing on a gallop away from the battle, further off to the left of the Persian flank. Fearful of being flanked, the Persians mimic his movement, sending their own cavalry to mirror Alexander's cavalry. Drawn away from the center are Darius' crack troops, the horsed noblemen that make up his cavalry arm. The center of the Persian line has been weakened and deprived of its best soldiers. They are spread thin.

The deathblow comes when Alexander wheels suddenly and breaks back toward the battlefield, charging hard toward the weakened Persian center. The Persian cavalry, surprised, are embroiled in combat with the light infantry that have kept pace with Alexander's forces, and are unable to check the Companion's advance. Unimpeded, the Companion cavalry crashes into the thin Persian line, splintering it, penetrating it, and ensuring victory even though bloody combat would continue for the rest of the day. This battle is one of the best examples in military history to illustrate how effective a spread offense can be.

In Alexander's great victory, the famous conqueror uses the tenets discussed throughout this book. He spread his own forces to thin the enemy's defense; he used deception and misdirection to draw the enemy's best soldiers away from the point of attack; and, when he finally committed his own forces to battle, the Macedonians outnumbered and outclassed the Persians at the point of attack.

An entire book can be written on the correlation between football and warfare, but it is sufficient for our purposes to see that there is a correlation, and that the basic tenets of the spread bone offense have been used by the world's greatest generals for millennia. Hopefully, your team can use these same tenets on the gridiron with equal success.

About the Authors

Heath Hamrick is a varsity receiver and defensive end coach at Rio Vista High School in Rio Vista, Texas. Prior to assuming his current position in 2005, Hamrick worked as a varsity assistant and history teacher at Saint Jo High School in Saint Jo, Texas from 2004 to 2005. Born in Pasadena, Texas, into a third-generation coaching family, Hamrick grew up on the sidelines as his father, Slugger Hamrick, coached at places ranging from Central Texas to the Rio Grande Valley and back again. An All-Brazos Valley selection both ways at Bremond (TX) High School, Hamrick played collegiate football—wide receiver and center—for Trinity University, where he won the inaugural Hustler of the Year award. Hamrick lives in Rio Vista, Texas, with his wife, Keri.

Todd Allen is a varsity assistant at Colony (5-A) High School in The Colony, Texas, a position he has held since 2004. Allen attended Trinity University, where he played quarterback and receiver for the Division III powerhouse Tigers. Following graduation, he spent a year as the head freshman coach for The Colony Cougars before moving up to the varsity staff. Allen and his wife, Morgan, live in the Lewisville, Texas, area.